LAGOM

The Swedish art of eating harmoniously

STEFFI KNOWLES-DELLNER

―――――――

Photography by Yuki Sugiura

quadrille

For TOBY *and* TOBBE

LAGOM [ˈlàːgɔm]: *adv. inte för mycket och
inte för lite, passande, lämpligt*

——

A Swedish word meaning "just the right amount;
enough, sufficient, adequate, just right"

Lagom is also widely translated as
"in moderation" and "in balance"

CONTENTS

INTRODUCTION

Over the past few years, the term "Scandi" has become a byword, a shorthand for a particular brand of minimal, effortless cool. And though our crime writers have a knack for depicting a land full of darkness and horror, in actuality Scandinavia is more often spoken about as a kind of utopia, an image bolstered by affirming statistics on health, equality and well-being. Sweden, in particular, is hailed as the ideal place to live and whenever I mention where I'm from people frequently sigh and respond: "they seem to have got so many things right over there".

When it comes to our food, however, few people seem to know very much about it beyond what can be found at IKEA. Perceptions seem to fall into one of two categories: either outlandish New Nordic gastronomy with a side of moss and ants or, at the opposite end of the spectrum, homely meatballs in cream sauce, beetroot and enough dill to fill a field.

This doesn't really paint a picture of the food that I grew up with or the meals that my Swedish family and friends cook back home. Sure, from time to time every Swede pines for some *husmanskost* – the traditional and thrifty home cooking that *mormor* (maternal granny) makes: salmon pudding, game stew, potato dumplings, oven-baked pancakes studded with crispy bacon and, yes, meatballs. But everyday Swedish food has evolved over the years, embracing a variety of ingredients, cultures, cooking styles and, above all, placing a much greater emphasis on balance and health.

LAGOM IS BEST

For me, the word that encapsulates the way we eat in Sweden is *lagom*. The Swedes themselves are the first to admit to their peculiar attachment to this small, loaded word, even to the extent of joking about how *lagom* they are. "Lagom är bäst" ("lagom is best"), they say, rolling their eyes.

Notoriously difficult to translate, *lagom* can be used to describe almost anything: you can be *lagom* well, your friend can be *lagom* tall, your coffee *lagom* strong and the weather *lagom* warm. But to dismiss it as simply a quantifier would be to underestimate its importance. *Lagom* goes right to the heart of Sweden's national psyche and characterizes everything from Sweden's political leanings and stance on gender equality to their aversion to anything too ostentatious. It is at the core of many typically Scandinavian ideals like fairness, consensus and equality.

And while this may sound like a doctrine of restraint, it is in fact anything but. *Lagom* is simply a manifestation of equilibrium – work and play, light and dark, hot and cold, wealth and poverty, tradition and modernity. You can find *lagom* in our distinctive seasons, our high taxes, understated design and deep appreciation of quality, innovation and progress, so long as it isn't too over-the-top or flashy – a bit like our sturdy Volvos and Saabs.

Not surprisingly, *lagom* extends to our cuisine as well – the Swedes take great pride in eating healthily, drawing on their own cooking traditions and the seasons' offerings. But they also know when it's time to break the rules and reach for a cinnamon bun or add a dash of sumac or chilli. Whether enough is as big as a feast or as small as breakfast, Swedes know how to celebrate life through food.

For us, eating has never been about extremes – swinging from one day to the next between excess and denial – but about harmony and enjoyment. Taking time to eat well, but also according to your means, the seasons and environment, while not shutting out pleasure or the rich food world beyond Scandinavia's borders – these are the core food philosophies that come naturally to Swedes.

THE NORDIC DIET

With their generous holiday allowances, extensive parental leave and work/life balance, there is time to spend in the kitchen, preparing more food from scratch. This is in part what contributes to a focus on health and eating well that is taken for granted in Sweden. Certainly, when I was growing up, overly sweet, processed food and drink did not enter the house: they simply didn't belong there. Instead, breakfasts were based around whole grains and dairy (often cultured products like *filmjölk*, a soured pouring yogurt) that set you up for the day; dinners always featured plenty of the hearty vegetables that grow in our cold climes; fish was enjoyed as often as meat; and puddings were treats that didn't make your teeth ache. Berries, rapeseed oil, root vegetables, nuts, rye, oily fish, game, unsweetened dairy products – these are the bread and butter of Scandinavian cooking and remain the staple ingredients in my kitchen today.

We'll put spelt flour into our cinnamon buns or even make them gluten- or dairy-free. We've become experts at sneaking goodness into our cakes and bakes by using a range of flours, adding nuts, seeds, fruit and even vegetables – something we've been doing long before it was trendy.

There are precedents for this. Many of our traditional baked goods were already relatively low in sugar; even our famous cinnamon buns are created from a cardamom-laced bread dough which only has a fraction of the sugar you would find in the UK equivalent. Our beloved pick 'n' mix is limited to one day,

known by every Swedish child as *lördagsgodis* – Saturday's Sweets.

A *lagom* approach recognizes that these little indulgences are important, vital even, in the celebration of life through food, but they are evened out by a varied diet, getting up and moving about and not overindulging. A little of what you fancy does you good and life is far too short not to eat cake...

LAGOM THROUGH THE SEASONS

This harmony can also be seen in the seasonal way that the Swedes eat. There is no shortage of Swedish holidays and festivities throughout the year, from the bonfires of *Walpurgis* Night in late April and Midsummer's Eve in June to St Lucia on 13th December. These are often marked with a specific food or dish. In fact, most Swedes even have a designated "name day" when you can expect a few cards and a slice of cake in honour of your name. Sometimes we celebrate food itself – National Cinnamon Bun Day on 4th October must surely be one of the best days of the year.

A knowledge of what is in season is deeply engrained in every Swede from an early age. Ever since I was old enough to walk, I was taught to pick ingredients (often from the wild) and recognize when they were ripe and ready. I grew up foraging for berries and whiling away afternoons fishing. We gathered bilberries, raspberries and dainty, perfumed wild strawberries in the late summer. In the spring, donning gardening gloves for protection, I snipped young nettles for soup, dandelion leaves for salads and plucked clove flowers, just to suck out the sweet nectar from the petals.

I grew up thinking that all this was part and parcel of life. For me, food became heavily associated with different times of the year and steeped in ritual. I'd gut herring with my mum before Midsummer's Eve, staying up late into the bright night to complete the task. In August I would steal one or, depending on how brazen I was feeling, two live crayfish from the crate for our annual crayfish party. I thought I was doing nature a good turn by "setting them free" in the sea. It wasn't until much later that I realized that releasing freshwater crayfish into the Baltic probably did them more harm than good.

It always seemed to me that everything we cooked in the summers I spent in the Stockholm archipelago was underpinned by an appreciation and respect for ingredients or *råvaror* (raw goods). Until relatively recently, there was a limit to what was available all year round in this far-flung, snow-capped corner of the world. So when lingonberry season came, the berries were relished in cakes and preserved in jams and cordials in order to enjoy them to their full but also ensure they lasted well into the colder months. And while foraging and preserving may not be a necessity any more, the ebb and flow of the Swedish calendar would simply not be the same without these foods to punctuate it.

Every year, my godmother, Margareta, feverishly hides the forest chanterelles she spots on her dog walks with leaves and branches. This shields them from other walkers so she can return and pick her plump, orange bounty when it is just right. The enjoyment of life through food is a serious business, but only because we know it is essential to have these events to look forward to and how important it is to mark a new season, another year. These small but significant acts help bring us together and acknowledge the passing of time.

A SMALL CORNER IN THE NORTH

The general perception of Swedish food is that it, like its geography, is fairly isolated from the rest of the world. But this couldn't be further from the truth. Swedes have been on the move since the 9th century, when the Vikings managed to get all the way to Constantinople and are said to have traded slaves for exotic spices like cinnamon and cardamom. These gradually worked their way into our own

baking and cooking traditions. More recently, we've been particularly influenced by other cultures, beginning with the mass emigration in the mid 19th century to the States and Canada, when extreme poverty saw increasing numbers make the journey across the Atlantic in the hope of a better life.

Even as late as the 1950s, my *mormor*'s best friend joined the thousands who moved to Canada in hope of prosperity after the war. They still write to each other regularly and she sometimes asks if I've heard of exotic Canadian recipes like *poutine* ("sounds horrible" according to *mormor*). But while her friend never returned to Sweden, many others eventually did, bringing with them new classics like hot dogs, pizza and other recipes shared amongst the hodgepodge of immigrants arriving in North America from Europe and Asia.

After the Second World War, Sweden also became a haven for many escaping a war-torn world. Initially, we saw arrivals from other Scandinavian countries (my paternal grandmother ended up marrying the first man who helped her with her luggage when she got off the boat from Helsinki), but later from all around the world. They brought with them their food heritage and came to shape the varied, rich food culture that gradually became Swedish as well. This is a tradition that remains strong to this day – in the past few years we have accepted more refugees per capita than any other European country.

Swedes themselves are extraordinarily well travelled. Even today, my relocation to London is hardly noteworthy back home. I am simply one of many who has put down roots abroad. And as our world view has widened, so has our appetite for new flavours and ways to enhance our own cooking. It always surprises people when I explain that tacos are a big deal in Sweden – in households around the country, every Friday, you will find families gathering round to assemble their tacos and hunker down in front of a film for *fredagsmys* (Friday cosy). We've also got our own take on *pierogi* (European dumplings), make raspberry and chocolate scones for breakfast, and add dill and tarragon to our pestos.

Swedes are notorious "early adopters" of trends, which in part explains why the healthy eating movement has been active there for so long. Meanwhile, in many Swedish cities the food truck revolution has brought kimchi burgers, sourdough pizzas and craft ales to the masses, and restaurants will offer everything from classic bistro fare to *ceviche*.

Part of a balanced way of eating now embraces other cultures more than ever. There is a pastiche of influences rooted in Swedish traditions, a reverence for ingredients, seasonality and a healthy attitude towards to eating. This is the kind of food philosophy that is at the heart of real Swedish cooking. It's not about perfection, but harmony. It is the unfussy food lovingly made in kitchens up and down this long country during the cold, dark winter months right through to the lengthy summer days when the sun never seems to set. Food that will look after you but is still full of life and joy – adventurous, wholesome dishes that satisfy even my insatiable appetite. There's so much more to it than just meatballs!

"Lagom är bäst" ["lagom is best"]

FRUKOST
[breakfast]

The Swedes are generally pretty early risers with the working day starting at 8A.M. – ideal when many aim to leave the office by late afternoon in time to pick up the kids from school. These early starts are particularly admirable given that for much of the year Swedes will wake up, have breakfast and go to work in complete darkness. The only way to get through these dispiriting winter mornings is to wrap up ("there's no such thing as bad weather, only bad clothing" as my *mormor* always says) and to fuel up, so a good breakfast is pretty essential. A typical Swedish breakfast combines whole grains with proteins like dairy, nuts and seeds, along with some fruit or vegetables for vitamins, fibre and sweetness. It should keep you full for hours but not be impossibly difficult to prepare. Weekends are a different matter, when time can be taken for a leisurely, more indulgent meal.

A favourite breakfast is a bowl of *filmjölk* or *fil*. This cultured yogurt product is a good source of protein and low in fat with a slightly sour taste. It can be served with any range of cereals, as well as acting as an ingredient in breads and cakes. I love it served cold in the summer with fresh fruit and muesli, ideally sat on a porch, barefoot, looking out to sea.

Another classic Swedish breakfast, certainly the most popular in cafés, is the open-face sandwich. These can be topped with cheese, ham or paté and normally a slice of veg – tomato, cucumber or pepper – and make for a quick and balanced way to start the day. Eggs can feature as well, usually served hard-boiled, sometimes with a squiggle of Kalles Kaviar (salted cod's roe from a tube) and a side of crispbread with cheese.

These breakfasts are enjoyed by the whole family – not much distinction is made between adults and children for this particular meal. And though it can of course be a hectic affair at times, breakfast is generally a chance for everyone to gather around the table and wake up, while scrambling for spreads and cartons before then heading off to work or school. The emphasis is on starting the day properly, with a good meal and as a unit. As my favourite line in Lukas Moodysson's cult film *Tillsammans* (*Together*) goes: "Better to eat porridge together than beef fillet alone".

There are few better ways to kick off the weekend than with a stack of pancakes. These ones are made with buckwheat flour, which is gluten-free and adds a wonderfully nutty flavour. Combined with the buttermilk and whisked egg whites, these are more souffléed than your average American variety. As such, they are a little more challenging to flip, but so worth the effort for their fluffy, cloud-like texture. For a sweeter version, omit the chives, add another tablespoon of maple syrup, and serve with berries.

Buckwheat, chive & lemon pancakes

———

with smoked salmon & crème fraîche

[YOU WILL NEED]

100g [¾ cup] buckwheat flour
½ tsp bicarbonate of soda [baking soda]
140ml [⅔ cup] *filmjölk* or buttermilk
3 eggs – 1 whole and 2 whites
1 tbsp pure maple syrup
small bunch of chives, chopped,
    plus extra to serve
1 lemon, zest and juice, plus extra
    wedges to serve
cold-pressed rapeseed oil or olive oil,
    for frying
smoked salmon, to serve
crème fraîche, to serve

[SERVES 4]
[MAKES 6–8 PANCAKES]

Put the flour and bicarbonate of soda in a large bowl with a pinch of salt. Whisk in the buttermilk, the whole egg and maple syrup, then add the chives, lemon zest and juice. Beat well to form a thick batter.

In a separate bowl, whisk the egg whites with electric beaters until thick, frothy and just holding their shape in soft peaks. Add one generous tablespoon to the batter, mixing well to lighten slightly. Using a metal spoon, carefully fold in the remaining whites, while taking care to keep as much air in the mixture as possible.

Heat a good glug of olive oil in your best non-stick frying pan and add a large spoonful of the batter, swirling with the spoon to create rounds. Once little bubbles start to appear on the surface, flip over – a palette knife will help with this. Leave for another minute or so then remove from the pan.

Serve straightaway or keep warm in a low oven while you crack on with the remaining batter. Serve the pancakes with some smoked salmon, a dollop of crème fraîche, a couple of lemon wedges and a sprinkle of chives.

The Swedes have a particular affinity with all things British – they love the music, the culture and they have a thing for afternoon tea. Baking scones for breakfast has been popular for quite some time back home and I have taken this one step further by turning them into a breakfast muffin. These have a similar texture to a scone with a crustier outside, but softer centre, which makes them perfect for spreading with toppings. Here, I have paired them with a quick, cheat's curd that may well be a bit less sweet than the jarred variety, but it's still a treat. The recipe will make enough for leftovers. Make a big batch of muffins and grab one when you are on the go. If you want a healthier serving suggestion, try a compote made by simmering your favourite fruit with a little vanilla extract and desired sweetener until soft.

Wholemeal scone-muffins

—

with grapefruit & pink pepper curd

[YOU WILL NEED]

For the curd
50g [3½ Tbsp] unsalted butter, softened
75g [6 Tbsp] caster [granulated] sugar
4 large eggs – 2 whole and 2 yolks
1 large pink grapefruit, zest and juice
½ tsp pink peppercorns, finely crushed

For the muffins
200g [1½ cups] wholemeal [whole-wheat] flour
1 Tbsp light muscovado sugar
1 tsp baking powder
½ tsp bicarbonate of soda [baking soda]
200ml [scant 1 cup] buttermilk or *filmjölk*
1 tsp vanilla extract
50g [3½ Tbsp] butter, melted and cooled slightly

[MAKES 1 JAR OF CURD
AND 9–10 SCONE-MUFFINS]

Begin by making the curd. Using electric beaters, beat the butter until creamy, then add the sugar and continue to whisk until light and fluffy. Whisk the eggs and yolks together in a jug with a fork, then gradually add to the sugar and butter, beating constantly. Carefully fold in the grapefruit juice, zest and peppercorns. The mixture may split, but don't worry, it will come together in the pan.

Pour the curd into a medium heavy-based saucepan and cook over a low heat, stirring constantly. As the mixture thickens, you can increase the heat a little until it coats the back of a spoon without dripping off (or reaches about 75°C/167°F, if you have a sugar thermometer). Pour into a sterilized jar and allow to cool completely.

Preheat the oven to 180°C/350°F and line two six-hole muffin tins. Combine the flour, sugar, baking powder and bicarbonate of soda with a pinch of salt in a large bowl. Whisk the buttermilk or *filmjölk* with the vanilla and cooled melted butter in a jug.

Make a well in the centre of the dry ingredients and pour in the buttermilk mixture. Mix to form a sticky dough; do not overmix. Divide between the muffin cases and bake for 20–25 minutes until risen and golden. Allow to cool slightly before turning out of the tin and serving with the curd.

Lingonberries, also known as cowberries, are jewel-like berries rich in antioxidants and vitamins. Most often they are used in jams which can be very sweet to compensate for their natural tartness, so I try to use the real article if I have it, but then I don't mind their sour, zingy flavour. If you are lucky enough to find frozen lingonberries from a specialist supplier, this is a great use for them. Of course, you can simply use lingonberry jam or substitute the berries for fresh or frozen cranberries. This breakfast is based on a kind of potato cake called råraka or raggmunk, which is normally served for dinner or lunch with bacon or sometimes whitefish roe, red onion and sour cream. I personally think it makes an excellent breakfast fritter for a lazy weekend brunch.

Crispy sweet potato cakes

—

with bacon & lingonberries

[YOU WILL NEED]

100g [3½oz] fresh or frozen lingonberries
    (or cranberries)
4 Tbsp maple syrup
1 onion
2 medium sweet potatoes [about
    300g/10½oz], peeled
2 thyme sprigs, leaves picked, plus extra
    to garnish
2 medium eggs, beaten
4 bacon rashers [slices]
2 tsp olive oil

[SERVES 2]

If using fresh or frozen lingonberries, add these to a small pan with the maple syrup and a splash of water. Simmer over a low heat until the fruit is soft and slightly jammy (5–10 minutes for frozen and more for fresh), then allow to cool.

Grate the onion and sweet potatoes coarsely and mix together in a large bowl with the thyme and eggs, then season generously with salt and pepper.

Either fry or grill [broil] the bacon, to your liking. Meanwhile, heat the oil in a frying pan and add spoonfuls of the sweet potato mixture, creating rounds about 8cm [3¼in] in diameter. You should have enough for 8 small cakes or 4 large ones. Fry over a medium-low heat until crisped up and golden before carefully flipping over, about 5 minutes on each side should do it. Garnish with thyme and serve with the crispy bacon and lingonberries.

PORRIDGE

Four recipes for the colder months

---

[1] Buckwheat & almond porridge with roasted plum & vanilla compote
[2] Spiced rye porridge with raspberries
[3] Indulgent oat porridge with brown butter & cream
[4] Coconut brown rice porridge with mango, lime & black sesame seeds

[ALL RECIPES SERVE 2]

Porridge's [oatmeal's] quick (even microwaveable) preparation and long list of nutritional credentials has made it a breakfast favourite the world over. In Sweden, it is often a winter weekday staple, but there is nothing to stop you from having pimped-up porridge at the weekend or taking a bit more time and care with it during the week.

Porridge has played a role in the Swedish diet since the days of the Vikings when it was based on different grains, flours and even an early form of *skyr* (an Icelandic dairy product similar to strained yogurt). Much later, a luxurious, thick rice porridge dusted with cinnamon became a regular feature at Christmas. To this day, Swedes will leave a bowl of porridge, often topped with butter, out for Santa. I imagine it's just the thing you need when you've got a whole globe's worth of presents to deliver.

I never grew up with the notion that porridge is always an entirely guilt-free breakfast. While I personally prefer a little more protein and fewer carbs to start the day, it can be the perfect, warming, comforting bowl that sometimes just hits the spot. When I was working in kitchens and would come home late from a long shift, frozen from the night-bus journey home, hungry and exhausted, porridge was all I wanted before hitting the hay.

My range of porridges includes some nice and some naughty and should see you through any of your cravings.

"Better to eat porridge together than beef fillet alone."
FROM THE FILM *TILSAMMANS* [*TOGETHER*, 2000]

This is a delicious, gluten-free porridge which I personally prefer warm. However, should you feel more adventurous, you can buy buckwheat groats and soak them overnight before blitzing with a little almond milk and some of the plum compote for a bircher-style version. The plum compote makes more than enough and should last for several days in the fridge, and is perfect as a topper for Greek yogurt (or ice cream).

1. Buckwheat & almond porridge

——

with roasted plum & vanilla compote

[YOU WILL NEED]

100g [generous ½ cup] buckwheat flakes
150ml [⅔ cup] milk or almond milk,
    plus extra to serve
1 banana, mashed well
2 Tbsp almonds, roughly chopped
¼ tsp almond extract (optional)
maple syrup, honey or sugar, to
    taste (optional)

For the compote
6 ripe plums
2 vanilla pods [beans], split lengthways
2 Tbsp maple syrup
1 Tbsp coconut oil or mild-flavoured oil

Start with the compote. Preheat the oven to 200°C/400°F and halve the plums, removing their stones. Use a small knife or a pair of kitchen scissors to cut them free if they are particularly stubborn. Place the plum halves on a roasting tray with the split vanilla pods, scraping out some of the seeds. Toss with the maple syrup and oil to coat completely then bake for 30–35 minutes until collapsing and beginning to caramelize. Scrape into a bowl and stir briefly until jammy.

Place all the ingredients for the porridge, except 1 tablespoon of the almonds, in a small pan along with 150ml [⅔ cup] water and a pinch of salt. Bring to a gentle simmer, then lower the heat and cook until thick, about 5–10 minutes, or until the flakes are cooked through and the porridge has reached the consistency you prefer.

To serve, divide the porridge between 2 bowls, pour over a little more milk and sweeten, if desired. Top with a few spoonfuls of compote and the reserved chopped almonds.

2. Spiced rye porridge

____

with raspberries

[YOU WILL NEED]

110g [scant 1 cup] rye flakes
250ml [1 cup] skimmed milk,
   plus extra to serve
½ tsp ground cinnamon
½ tsp ground ginger
1 tsp ground cardamom
pinch of chilli powder (optional)
raspberries, to serve
honey, to serve

Place the rye flakes, milk and 350ml [1½ cups] water in a medium saucepan along with the spices. Slowly bring to a gentle simmer, stirring frequently. Let the porridge bubble away, adding more water if necessary, for about 20–25 minutes until the rye is cooked through and creamy.

Serve with the raspberries and some more milk, and sweeten with honey, if desired.

3. Indulgent oat porridge

____

with brown butter & cream

[YOU WILL NEED]

2 Tbsp unsalted butter
100g [1 cup] rolled oats
200ml [scant 1 cup] milk
1 Tbsp oat bran (optional)
sugar, honey or sweetener, to taste
   (optional)
single [light] cream, to serve

Begin by melting the butter in a large saucepan over a medium heat and cooking until browned and nutty smelling. This should take a few minutes, but do keep an eye on it as the milk solids will burn if left too long. Set aside 1 teaspoon or so of the melted butter, then add the oats to the pan and stir through, gently toasting for a few minutes.

Pour in the milk and 300ml [1¼ cups] water and a pinch of salt. Add the oat bran, if using, then bring to a simmer and cook for 12–15 minutes until soft and oozy. Sweeten if desired, then serve drizzled with cream and the reserved butter.

My dad always makes a rich, creamy rice porridge for dessert on Christmas Eve, a Swedish custom since the late 19th century. Back then, a single blanched almond was placed in the porridge pot with the promise of marriage within the year for the recipient. I've always found this traditional way to make rice porridge a little too rich for my taste (not least when fried in butter and sprinkled with cinnamon as my father does with the leftovers), but rice can still make a wonderful base for breakfast. This zesty coconut version gets my vote for starting the day.

4. Coconut brown rice porridge

——

with mango, lime & black sesame seeds

[YOU WILL NEED]

150g [¾ cup] short-grain brown rice
400ml [1¾ cups] coconut milk
1 cinnamon stick
3 cardamom pods, ground
½ tsp vanilla paste or a pinch
    vanilla powder
1 lime, juice of 1 and zest of ½
sugar, honey or sweetener, to taste
    (optional)
1 small mango, peeled, stoned and sliced
2 tsp black sesame or poppy seeds
1 tsp flaked or desiccated [shredded
    unsweetened] coconut

Begin by cooking the rice according to the packet instructions. You can also use leftover rice, as long as it has been cooled and stored properly in the fridge.

Combine the rice, coconut milk, cinnamon stick, cardamom and vanilla in a large saucepan with a pinch of salt. Slowly bring to a simmer, stirring occasionally, for about 10–15 minutes until the coconut milk has reduced and the porridge is creamy. Add a splash of water or milk if you take it too far.

Remove the cinnamon stick, stir through the lime zest and juice and sweeten with your favourite sweetener, if desired. Divide between 2 bowls, top with the mango slices and sprinkle over the sesame seeds and coconut.

Sometimes a freshly baked crusty roll is the only thing that will do and I think if you are going to allow yourself a much derided bit of white bread, nothing beats home-baked. These are called 7A.M. rolls because they can be made the morning that you want to eat them – start at 7 and they will be done by breakfast at 9A.M. There's no kneading and you don't need to wait for them to rise once they have been shaped. The recipe is adapted from a wonderful book, Vinterns goda ting by Anna and Fanny Bergenström. They are crusty, fluffy rolls that can be eating still warm from the oven, spread with butter and jam.

7A.M. breakfast rolls

—

with sour cherry & vanilla jam

[YOU WILL NEED]

25g [1oz] fresh yeast
1 Tbsp honey
70g [½ cup] wholemeal [whole-wheat] flour
700g [5 cups] strong white bread flour, plus extra for dusting and sprinkling

For the jam
400g [14oz] fresh or frozen sour cherries (or black cherries if sour are not available), stoned
½ lemon
1 vanilla pod [bean], split in half lengthways
150g [¾ cup] golden caster [unrefined granulated] sugar

[MAKES 8]

Crumble the yeast into a large bowl with the honey and 1 teaspoon salt and mix until the yeast dissolves. Pour in 600ml [2½ cups] "finger warm" (just warm to touch) water and mix thoroughly. Add the flours and mix together with a wooden spoon to form a sticky dough, but don't knead.

Cover the bowl with a tea towel and allow to rise for about an hour.

Meanwhile, make the jam. Place the cherries, a squeeze of lemon juice and vanilla pod in a small pan with 1 large spoonful of the sugar. Bring to a gentle simmer and stir until the sugar dissolves. Add another spoonful of sugar and repeat, continuing until all the sugar has been used up. Simmer for 20–30 minutes until jammy. You can use the wrinkle test with a cold plate to see if it is done (see note opposite). Then pour into a sterilized jar.

Preheat the oven to 220°C/425°F and lightly grease 2 baking sheets. Tip the dough out onto a floured work surface and flatten, sprinkling over with plenty of flour – this will make the dough easier to handle. Using a table knife or a dough scraper, divide the dough into 8 pieces and shape into about 8–10-cm [3¼–4-in] rounds. Transfer onto the prepared baking sheets, spacing out evenly.

Sprinkle over a little extra flour, then bake for 17–19 minutes until risen and golden. Allow to cool a little before getting stuck in, slathering with the jam.

*NOTE the wrinkle test

Before starting the jam, place a saucer in the freezer. To test if the jam is ready, place a teaspoon onto the ice-cold plate and leave for a minute or so to cool completely. Push a finger across the jam. If it wrinkles, the jam is ready, but if it is still too liquid, keep cooking for a bit longer.

It would be remiss of me not to include at least one egg recipe in this book, as a boiled egg is such a staple on the Swedish breakfast table. I also wanted to celebrate our love of mushrooms, particularly in late summer/early autumn when they are there for the picking in forests and fields – with the right knowledge, of course. This breakfast is a wonderfully savoury way to start the day. Omit the garlic if you find it too much first thing. Personally, I like to add more.

Chanterelle toast

——

with poached eggs & kale

[YOU WILL NEED]

2 handfuls of kale, stalks removed and
    leaves torn into bits
1 Tbsp cold-pressed rapeseed oil or
    olive oil, plus a little extra for drizzling
100g [3½oz] chanterelle mushrooms,
    or mixed wild mushrooms, torn
    into chunks
1 garlic clove, very finely chopped
1 small handful of parsley, roughly
    chopped
2 large eggs
1 Tbsp white wine vinegar
2 slices of sourdough bread

[SERVES 2]

Bring a large pan of water to the boil. Blanch the kale for a minute or two, then remove with a slotted spoon and drain, squeezing out any excess water. Keep the water simmering while you crack on with the mushrooms.

Heat the oil in a large saucepan and add the mushrooms, taking care not to overcrowd them. Fry for 4–5 minutes until golden and softened.

Add the garlic to the pan and fry for a minute until no longer fragrant. Add the kale and stir through for a minute or two until all of the water has evaporated and the leaves starts to crisp up, about 5 minutes. Season with salt and pepper and sprinkle in most of the parsley.

Meanwhile, crack the eggs into a couple of ramekins or cups. Add the vinegar to the pan of simmering water and swirl with a spoon to create a whirlpool. Hold the ramekin close to the surface of the water and quickly tip one egg into the swirling water. Increase the heat slightly and poach the egg for 2 minutes until set. Remove and set aside while you repeat with the other egg.

Toast the sourdough and drizzle with a little more oil. Divide the mushrooms and kale between the toasts, then top with the poached eggs. Sprinkle with a little more parsley and a good grinding of black pepper.

Baked eggs

with lumpfish roe, shallots & dill

[YOU WILL NEED]

4 tsp butter, plus a little extra for greasing
2 banana shallots, sliced
4 large eggs
3–4 Tbsp half-fat crème fraîche
2 tsp capers, finely chopped
1 small handful of dill, chopped
4 tsp black or red lumpfish roe, to serve
toast, to serve

[SERVES 4]

Preheat the oven to 200°C/400°F and boil the kettle. Melt the butter in a medium frying pan and cook the shallots until soft and translucent, about 5 minutes.

Grease 4 ramekins with a little extra butter. Crack an egg into each, then divide the crème fraîche, fried shallots, capers and most of the dill among them. Season with salt and pepper.

Place the ramekins in a roasting tray and carefully pour hot water into the tray until it comes about halfway up the ramekins. Bake for 10–12 minutes until the egg whites have just set and the yolks still have a bit of a wobble. Sprinkle with the remaining dill and serve each with a teaspoon of lumpfish roe and some toast.

Buttermilk breakfast bowl

with crispbread

[YOU WILL NEED]

200ml [scant 1 cup] *filmjölk* (similar to buttermilk), pouring yogurt or *skyr* mixed with a little milk
1 large handful of crispbread, broken up into chunks
ground cinnamon, to serve
sugar, to serve

[SERVES 1]

This is so simple and hardly a recipe. I struggle to find a breakfast cereal that I like – I find most commercially available cereals far too sweet. Crispbread, however, is always to hand, inexpensive and satisfyingly crunchy.

Pour the *filmjölk* or yogurt mixture into a bowl. Top with crispbread and sprinkle with cinnamon and sugar, if desired. Done.

Berry bircher muesli

with almonds

[YOU WILL NEED]

2 generous handfuls of raspberries
100g [1 cup] oat, wheat or rye flakes,
    or a mixture
200ml [scant 1 cup] skimmed milk
1 apple
2 Tbsp almonds, roughly chopped
2 Tbsp sultanas or raisins
4 Tbsp Greek yogurt, to serve
blueberries, blackberries and raspberries,
    to serve

[SERVES 2]

Place the raspberries in a large bowl and lightly squish with a fork. Add the flakes and milk and mix together well. Place in the fridge overnight to soak.

In the morning, grate the apple into the bircher and mix well. Stir through the almonds and sultanas or raisins, then divide between 2 bowls. Dollop over a little Greek yogurt and serve with the berries.

Almond skyr

with grilled peaches & lemon balm

[YOU WILL NEED]

2 peaches or nectarines, halved and
    stoned
2 tsp butter
300g [1¼ cups] *skyr* or Greek yogurt
2 Tbsp ground almonds
vanilla paste, to taste
few lemon balm or mint sprigs, to serve

[SERVES 2]

Heat a griddle pan for 2 minutes and place the peach halves on top, cut side down. After a minute, flip over and place the butter in the holes. Grill for another few minutes, then transfer to a plate to cool slightly.

Mix the *skyr* or yogurt, almonds and vanilla together, then divide between 2 bowls.

Top with the peaches and sprinkle over a few lemon balm leaves. Eat while the peaches are still hot.

As I have mentioned, breakfast cereals are a challenge for me. Too many of them are tooth-achingly sweet and send me doolally before I ultimately hit a wall of hunger after a few hours. I also want to taste the earthiness of the grains, nuttiness of the seeds and every so often, just get a kick of sweetness from a bit of dried fruit, but certainly not in every bite. This granola ticks each and every one of these boxes. The dates are the primary sticky, clumping agent as without lots of sugar or oil it won't cluster in quite the same way as commercial granola, but you will still have plenty of crunch and a good dose of toasty warmth. Serve it sparingly with real Greek yogurt or skyr and fresh fruit for a bushy-tailed way to start the day.

Autumn granola

—

with hazelnuts, rye, spelt & dates

[YOU WILL NEED]

75g [¾ cup] spelt flakes
100g [generous ¾ cup] rye flakes
150g [1½ cups] rolled oats
30g [¼ cup] sunflower seeds
30g [¼ cup] pumpkin seeds
100g [¾ cup] blanched hazelnuts,
   roughly chopped
30g [scant ¼ cup] flaxseeds
½ tsp ground cardamom
1 tsp ground cinnamon
good grating of nutmeg
2 Tbsp rice malt syrup (or honey
   or maple syrup)
1 Tbsp coconut oil, melted
75g [½ cup] pitted chopped dates
Greek yogurt or *skyr*, to serve
berries of your choice, to serve

[MAKES 1 LARGE JAR]

Preheat the oven to 200°C/400°F and line 2 baking sheets with baking parchment. Combine all the ingredients, except the dates, in a large bowl with a pinch of salt and stir well, dispersing everything evenly.

Divide the granola between the baking sheets and bake for 10 minutes. Toss the ingredients a bit and swap oven shelves. Continue to toast for a further 5–10 minutes, until golden and crisping up slightly. Allow to cool completely before adding the dates and transferring to an airtight container. The granola will last for up to a month in a cool place.

Serve with Greek yogurt and berries, such as blueberries and blackberries.

LÄTTARE RÄTTER
[lunches, sides & light bites]

While weekends are a more relaxed, casual affair in Sweden, during the week lunchtime acts as a proper pause from work, to be respected and observed, even during busy times. As the working day typically begins quite early, lunch breaks can start before noon, but this is becoming less common as more continental eating and working practices are gradually being adopted.

The preference is for a large, hot meal in the middle of the day and so lunch specials are very common in restaurants and cafés. This typically consists of a main dish, some bread and salad, as well as a drink and/or cup of coffee, and perhaps a cookie if you are lucky. It's generally a good deal and a great tip for tourists visiting what can be an expensive country. My favourite is crispy fried herring with mash, lingonberries and a cold *lättöl* (low-alcohol beer – not much fun but good if you've got things to do in the afternoon).

Having said that, there is also a growing appetite for lighter, more health-conscious dishes – salads, fish, open-faced sandwiches and soups. The emphasis, however, is always on a proper break and on proper food. It's about separating yourself from your work and getting away from your desk to feel restored and revived.

The dishes in this chapter are just that. Many are flexible enough to act as sides with leftovers from last night's dinner and simply need a little salad and chunk of bread to make a full meal packed up for lunch. There are also some options for weekends when there is more time to cook and several could work as a starter or snack, like the open sandwiches or the cod paté.

"Låt maten tysta mun"
["Let the food shut the mouth"]
SWEDISH SAYING

This would make a lovely side dish as part of Sunday lunch or a dinner gathering. However, it holds its own as a simple weekday supper too, accompanied by nothing more than a green salad with a sharp vinaigrette and glass of dry white wine.

Sweet potato & leek gratin

——

with oat crumble topping

[YOU WILL NEED]

50g [3½ Tbsp] butter, plus extra
   for greasing
3 leeks, thinly sliced
2 garlic cloves, crushed
a few thyme sprigs, leaves picked
750g [1lb 10oz] sweet potatoes
150ml [⅔ cup] hot vegetable
   stock [broth]
100ml [7 Tbsp] double [heavy] cream
60g [scant ⅔ cup] oats
2 Tbsp wholemeal [whole-wheat] flour
2 Tbsp grated Parmesan

[SERVES 4 AS A MAIN MEAL
OR 6 AS A SIDE]

Preheat the oven to 180°C/350°F. Melt 30g [2 Tbsp] of the butter in a large frying pan. Add the leeks and sweat over a medium-high heat until softened but not coloured, about 10–15 minutes, stirring frequently. Add the garlic and thyme and continue to cook for a further few minutes until no longer pungent. Remove the pan from the heat.

Grease a roughly 20-cm [8-in] square/round ovenproof dish with a little butter. Peel the sweet potatoes and slice thinly, either using a mandoline (for the brave) or a knife (for the sensible). Arrange about a third of the potato slices on the base of the dish, then add about half of the leek mixture. Repeat, finishing with a final layer of sweet potato.

Combine the hot stock and cream in a jug, season generously and pour evenly over the dish.

Mix the oats, the remaining butter, flour and Parmesan together in a bowl, using your hands to form a crumbly mixture. Sprinkle over the sweet potato slices and bake for about 35–40 minutes, until golden and all the layers are cooked through when tested with a knife.

This is my Swedish take on a Mediterranean classic. The Greek yogurt and avocado give it a wonderfully creamy texture and trick you into thinking you are having something really quite rich and indulgent when actually this is a fresh and light dish with a major focus on veg. Add the chillies according to your taste – they vary a lot, so do taste a little before deciding. I prefer a decent kick.

Creamy cucumber & dill gazpacho

with pea salsa & sumac

[YOU WILL NEED]

1 cucumber, roughly chopped
2 yellow [bell] peppers, roughly chopped
1–2 green chillies (depending on taste),
   finely chopped
½ garlic clove, very finely chopped
2 spring onions [scallions], roughly
   chopped
3 Tbsp extra virgin olive oil
1 avocado, stoned, peeled and cubed
200g [scant 1 cup] Greek yogurt,
   plus extra to serve
1 small bunch of mint, roughly chopped
1 small bunch of dill, roughly chopped
pinch of sugar, or to taste
sumac, for sprinkling

For the salsa
100g [generous ¾ cup] frozen peas
½ red onion, finely chopped
1 lemon, zest and juice

[SERVES 4]

Blitz the cucumber, peppers, chillies, garlic, spring onions, 2 tablespoons of the oil and all but 1 tablespoon of the cubed avocado together in a food processor. Add the yogurt and most of the herbs and continue to blend until smooth. Season with salt, pepper and sugar to taste. Add a little water if the soup seems too thick.

Blanch the peas in a pan of boiling water for just a minute, then refresh in cold water. Drain thoroughly, then mix with the red onion, lemon juice and zest, remaining oil and reserved avocado. Sprinkle in any leftover herbs.

To serve, pour into chilled bowls and top with a dollop of yogurt, the pea salsa and a sprinkling of sumac.

Autumn and winter can be a tricky time for salads, particularly when there is a dearth of crisp, ripe vegetables. Even a straightforward tomato can be a flavourless, watery disappointment. But winter leaves can make for unexpected and tasty lettuce replacements. Kale has received excellent press in recent years, but few seem to know that it can be eaten raw in salads. It just needs the help of a brief but firm massage to break down some of its toughness.

An autumn salad

---

with massaged kale, spelt, dried cranberries, lime & hazelnuts

[YOU WILL NEED]

250g [1⅔ cups] pearled spelt
50g [generous ⅓ cup] blanched hazelnuts
1 large bag of kale, ideally a mixture
   of green and purple leaves
1 lime, juice
30g [¼ cup] dried cranberries

For the dressing
½ apple, peeled and cored
3 Tbsp extra virgin olive oil
1 tsp cider vinegar
few thyme sprigs, leaves picked

[SERVES 4]

Bring a large pan of salted water to the boil. Add the spelt and simmer for about 20–25 minutes, or according to the packet instructions, until al dente. Briefly rinse under cold water and drain thoroughly.

Toast the hazelnuts in a dry frying pan over a medium heat. Stir or toss frequently until golden all over. Tip onto a plate and allow to cool completely, then roughly chop.

Tear the kale into small leafy pieces, discarding any thick woody stems. Place in a large bowl along with the lime juice and a generous pinch of salt. Gently massage the leaves for a few minutes, until they start to break down. You will notice a gradual change in colour as they tenderize. This takes a little while – keep tasting the leaves to see if they have softened. Add the spelt, cranberries and hazelnuts and toss together.

For the dressing, blitz the apple, olive oil and vinegar in a food processor, along with a pinch of salt and some ground black pepper. Finally, add the thyme leaves and blitz for another few seconds. Use to dress the salad.

Västerbotten is a classic Swedish cheese with a sharp, peppery flavour and very crumbly texture. It is often used in flavoursome quiches topped with lumpfish roe. It is becoming much more widely available, but if you can't find it, a really strong Cheddar will do the job. I do realize this is basically lettuce with a lettuce dressing but trust me on this one – it works.

Iceberg wedge salad

——

with västerbotten *& watercress dressing*

[YOU WILL NEED]

1 head of iceberg lettuce, base trimmed
    and any rough outer leaves removed
2 Tbsp pumpkin seeds

For the dressing
2 tsp cold-pressed rapeseed oil or olive oil
2 banana shallots, sliced
1 bag watercress (about 125g/4½oz)
100g [generous 1 cup] grated *västerbotten*
    cheese, or a mature [sharp] Cheddar,
    plus a little extra to serve
100ml [scant ½ cup] buttermilk (or 50ml/
    ¼ cup milk mixed with 50g/¼ cup
    Greek yogurt)

[SERVES 4 AS A SIDE OR
STARTER OR 2 FOR LUNCH]

Begin by making the dressing. Heat the oil in a saucepan and fry the shallots until soft and starting to caramelize, about 10 minutes over a low heat. Tip onto a plate to cool a little.

Bring a large pan of water to the boil and blanch the watercress for 30 seconds. Strain and run under the tap to cool down, then place in a tea towel and squeeze out as much liquid as possible.

Blitz the watercress with the shallots, cheese, buttermilk and some seasoning in a food processor or with a stick blender.

Cut the iceberg into thick wedges and drizzle over the dressing. Scatter with pumpkin seeds and a few extra shavings of cheese.

White asparagus starts to make an appearance around spring time and is one of those ingredients that causes a ripple of excitement among chefs. The stalks are grown underground without access to sunlight, giving them their pale colour and extra-tender texture. They can lend a bit of elegance to your meal (if you can find them) though you could, of course, use thick green asparagus stalks instead. Either way, this is a recipe to really celebrate this sprightly vegetable when it is at its very best.

Hazelnut-roasted white asparagus

with whipped goat's cheese, honey & thyme dip

[YOU WILL NEED]

500g [1lb 2oz] white asparagus (or green if unavailable – use the thick spears)
1 Tbsp hazelnut or walnut oil
30g [¼ cup] blanched hazelnuts
120g [½ cup] crème fraîche
55g [2oz] rindless goat's cheese
½ garlic clove, very finely chopped
2 tsp honey
few thyme sprigs, leaves picked and roughly chopped

[SERVES 4]

Preheat the oven to 220°C/425°F. Bring a large pan of water to the boil and blanch the asparagus for no more than a minute. Drain thoroughly, then tip into a roasting tin. Drizzle over the oil, scatter over the hazelnuts and season with salt and pepper. Toss everything together with your hands to coat.

Roast for 8–10 minutes, turning halfway through, until the asparagus starts to crisp up and feels soft when pierced with a knife.

Meanwhile, use a fork to mash the crème fraîche, goat's cheese and garlic together with a pinch of sea salt until creamy. Add the honey, most of the thyme leaves and mix everything together thoroughly then taste to adjust the seasoning. You can also blend the mixture for a smoother dip. Serve with the warm roasted asparagus spears, either as a dip or a drizzle, and sprinkle a few thyme leaves on top.

My very first job the summer I turned 16 was working in the kitchen of a fish stall of Östermalmshallen – a famous covered market selling only the finest produce to the most discerning Stockholmers (and those with the deepest pockets). My job was not particularly glamorous – the first task of each day was to pané hundreds of herring fillets in breadcrumbs. They arrived in boxes of ice and by the time I was finished, my hands would be red raw and completely numb. I remember so well that I was never trusted to season them. Instead, the head chef would come over and douse them in salt, pepper and dill. I would then sandwich the fillets together, ready for frying and finally divvying up into containers. Of course, I had to have a recipe for fried herring here, but instead of a traditional take, I have gone for a fresher twist. Season liberally and at will.

Lemon & rye-crumbed herring

—

stuffed with pine nuts & served with parsley aïoli

[YOU WILL NEED]

1 lemon, zest and juice
3 Tbsp olive oil
2 Tbsp pine nuts, toasted and roughly
   chopped
1 small bunch of parsley, finely chopped
50g [½ cup] rye flour
500g [1lb 2oz] herring, filleted and
   pin-boned (ask your fishmonger)

For the aïoli
2 egg yolks
1 garlic clove, very finely chopped
1 tsp Dijon mustard
200ml [scant 1 cup] sunflower oil

[SERVES 4]

Place the lemon juice, 1 tablespoon of the olive oil, the chopped pine nuts and parsley in a small bowl and mix together to form a chunky paste. Season with salt and pepper.

Mix the rye flour with the lemon zest and some seasoning in a shallow bowl. Coat the skin sides only, of half of the herring fillets with the rye flour mixture, then transfer to a baking sheet, uncoated sides up. Divide the parsley and pine-nut paste over the exposed fillets.

Coat the skin sides of the remaining fish with the rest of the rye flour mixture, then sandwich together with the other fillets so that the filling is in the middle. Refrigerate while you make the aïoli.

Mix the egg yolks, garlic and mustard together in a large bowl. Season, then, using electric beaters, whisk in the sunflower oil in a thin, steady stream. The mayonnaise should be quite thick, but do feel free to add a splash of water if you want a smoother consistency.

Heat the remaining olive oil in a large saucepan and fry the fish over a medium heat for about 5 minutes on both sides until completely cooked through. Serve with the aïoli.

As part of a wedding present, we were given something called "Viking Salt" by our friends, Hattie and Oli. It's basically a salt flavoured with a mild curry and I put it on everything. It may seem a peculiar spice for the Scandinavians to lay claim to, but we have flirted with unusual flavours for hundreds of years, sourced on those far-flung Viking plunders and raids. We use them gently, as a way to lightly season and add subtle layers of depth. This chunky soup is a perfect example. My mormor (maternal granny) has been making it for as long as I can remember. She only uses curry powder in the soup itself, but I also like to make a fragrant oil, swirled through at the end. For a lighter soup, use milk instead of cream and add a dollop of crème fraîche.

Mormor's curried fish soup

—

with curry oil

[YOU WILL NEED]

1 tsp butter
2 onions, thinly sliced
1 leek, sliced
2 garlic cloves, very finely chopped
2 tsp medium curry powder
1 litre [4½ cups] fish or vegetable
   stock [broth]
300g [10½oz] thick cod fillets, cut
   into chunks
300g [10½oz] salmon, cut into pieces
150g [5¼oz] cooked frozen Atlantic
   prawns [shrimp], defrosted
250ml [1 cup] single [light] cream
2 Tbsp cold-pressed rapeseed oil or
   olive oil
1 small bunch of dill, roughly chopped,
   to serve
1 small bunch of parsley, roughly
   chopped, to serve
chunky bread, to serve

[SERVES 4]

Melt the butter in a large saucepan, add the onions and sauté over a low heat for 5 minutes, without colouring. Add the leek and cook for another few minutes until softened, then add the garlic. Stir through 1 teaspoon of the curry powder and fry for another minute or so, until fragrant.

Pour in the stock, bring to the boil, then reduce the heat – it should be just quivering. Add the white fish and salmon and poach for 5–8 minutes, then tip in the prawns and continue to cook for 3 minutes. Remove from the heat and stir in the cream.

Heat the oil in a small frying pan and add the remaining curry powder. Fry for 1 minute or so until smoky and aromatic, then remove from the heat and tip into a bowl to cool slightly.

Divide the soup between 4 bowls, drizzle over a little curry oil and sprinkle with the herbs before serving with chunky bread.

The kind of pumpkins commonly sold in the UK should only really be used for Halloween carving as they are fairly flavourless to cook with. I am always on the lookout for interesting varieties of squash – try a smaller, knobbly, strange-looking one next time and taste your way forward until you find your favourite. This dressing is a rather Scandi take on pesto – using some of our favourite herbs in place of basil and our dearest nut, almond, instead of pine nuts.

Roasted pumpkin

———

with parsley, dill, tarragon & almond pesto

[YOU WILL NEED]

1 pumpkin or squash, such as butternut, coquina, kabocha or delicata, cut into wedges (seeds scooped out)
4 Tbsp cold-pressed rapeseed oil or olive oil
few thyme sprigs, leaves picked
2 Tbsp blanched almonds
1 lemon, zest and juice
1 small bunch each of parsley, dill and tarragon, leaves picked
1 Tbsp capers
pinch of sugar
1 Tbsp sesame seeds

[SERVES 4]

Preheat the oven to 200°C/400°F. Place the pumpkin or squash wedges on a baking sheet and drizzle over half the oil. Scatter over some thyme and season with sea salt and pepper. Roast for 30–40 minutes until soft when pierced with a knife and beginning to brown.

Meanwhile, toast the almonds in a dry frying pan until golden and starting to release some of their oils. Tip onto a plate to cool.

Add a little squeeze of lemon juice with the zest, most of the herbs and the remaining olive oil to a blender. Blitz until the herbs have broken up, then tip in the almonds, capers, sugar and some salt and pepper and continue to whizz, adding water if it's too thick, until you have a paste. Arrange the pumpkin on a serving platter and drizzle with the sauce. Sprinkle with the sesame seeds and any remaining herbs and serve while still warm, or at room temperature if you prefer.

As much as I love salt cod, I don't necessarily have the time or inclination to soak the dehydrated fillets before making into a brandade-style spread. This recipe skirts around the issue, with a slightly different texture and milder flavour, but still creamy and fishy enough to satisfy this very particular craving. Serve as a starter or for a light lunch.

Cod pâté with chives

——

on toasted rye bread

[YOU WILL NEED]

200g [7oz] cod fillets
½ lemon, zest and juice
2 garlic cloves
1 Tbsp cold-pressed rapeseed oil or olive
   oil, plus a little extra for drizzling
3 Tbsp single [light] cream
1 small bunch of chives, roughly chopped
rye or pumpernickel bread, toasted,
   to serve

[SERVES 4 AS A STARTER
OR 2 FOR LUNCH]

Preheat the oven to 200°C/400°F. Place the cod on a sheet of foil, squeeze over a little lemon juice and season. Fold up to create a tightly sealed parcel. Place on a baking sheet with the garlic cloves next to the parcel, drizzling these with the tiniest amount of oil, and bake for 20 minutes until the fish is cooked through and the garlic is soft.

Carefully remove the cod from the parcel and flake into a blender, taking care to discard any bones. Add the garlic by squeezing it out of its papery skin, along with any juices from the parcels to the blender. Add the cream, 1 tablespoon oil and half the chives. Blitz to a chunky consistency and stir though the remaining chives and the lemon zest. Season to taste with salt, pepper and lemon juice.

Serve sprinkled with more chives and a drizzle of oil, accompanied by toasted rye bread.

Hasselback potatoes are a firm favourite of the Swedish culinary canon, particularly as part of a special meal – I particularly like them served with game. However, they are quite fiddly and time-consuming so I find this recipe easier than faffing about with each individual potato. Not least as there is plenty of margin for error – any scrappy off-cuts can be tucked into the bake. You still get that crispy, crunchy texture in this version as well as a hit of freshness from the lemon. Serve as a side with a roast dinner or with a salad for a main meal.

Crispy sliced & stacked lemon-roasted potatoes

———

[*My hasselback bake*]

[YOU WILL NEED]

1.3–1.5kg [3–3¼lb] floury [mealy]
   potatoes, peeled
50ml [3½ Tbsp] olive oil
3 garlic cloves, very finely chopped
1½ lemons, zest and juice
1 tsp dried thyme
1 tsp dried oregano
2 thyme sprigs, leaves picked

[SERVES 4-6]

Begin by thinly slicing the potatoes, about ¼cm [⅛in] thick. The easiest way to do this is to use a mandoline or the slicing attachment on a food processor. If you are doing it by hand, make sure you have the radio on and a comfortable seat as it will take a while. Place the slices in a large bowl of cold water as you go.

Preheat the oven to 200°C/400°F. Drain the potatoes and pat very dry. Next, stack the potato slices lengthways and upright in a large ovenproof dish with high sides, about 35 x 20cm [14 x 10in], so the cut sides are facing you. Pack them tightly so that they support each other to form long rows.

Mix the olive oil, garlic, lemon juice and zest with the dried thyme and oregano. Drizzle over the potatoes, then sprinkle with sea salt and the fresh thyme.

Bake for 1 hour–1 hour 10 minutes, until crispy and golden. Cover with foil if the potatoes start going too brown. Be sure to test that the potato slices are cooked through with a skewer before removing from the oven.

SCANDI BRUSCHETTA

Five recipes for open sandwiches

---

[1] Purple sprouting broccoli with walnuts, capers & anchovies
[2] Butter beans with tarragon & chives
[3] Prawn & avocado with radishes & mustard
[4] Peas & broad beans with dill, mint & halloumi
[5] Fennel-crusted mackerel on crispbread with potatoes and fresh cheese

[ALL RECIPES SERVE 4]

Although the Danes are most famous for their open-faced sandwiches or *smørrebrød*, the Swedes love them too. In fact, we love sandwiches so much we even created a cake in dedication to them. The sandwich cake is often served to feed a crowd for a celebration, but it's really a party in itself. Sandwich cakes are normally "iced" with a mayonnaise and crème fraîche mixture and heavily decorated with anything and everything you can imagine but often hinting at what might lie beneath: prawns, ham, cheese, tomatoes, cress, herbs, lemon slices and even fruit – the possibilities are endless. There really are no limits when it comes to our dedication to this humble food.

As for the everyday sarnie, often called a *macka* or *smörgås*, we have them mostly for breakfast, and they are almost always open-faced and interesting. By this I mean that they aren't simply a bit of butter and a slice of ham and cheese on a thin piece of white bread – there should be more love and thought put into them. A leaf or two of curly lettuce, a round of sliced pepper and some cucumber delicately positioned – a well-made, open-faced sandwich can look like a work of art. As for the type of bread, rolls are preferable, but crispbread, rye bread and sourdough are also acceptable. Think of them as a Swedish bruschetta with endless possibilities.

I like the idea of these becoming a meal in themselves but I particularly like the thought of a selection being served for dinner as a starter or nibbles at a party.

"Att glida in på en räkmacka"
["To glide in on a prawn sandwich", i.e. to have it easy without any effort]

1. Purple sprouting broccoli

———

with walnuts, capers & anchovies

[YOU WILL NEED]

300g [10½oz] purple sprouting broccoli
50g [3½ Tbsp] butter, softened
4 anchovy fillets, finely chopped
3 Tbsp walnuts
2 Tbsp extra virgin olive oil
1 Tbsp sherry vinegar
4 slices of your favourite bread
2 Tbsp capers, roughly chopped
1 small bunch of parsley, roughly chopped

Steam the broccoli until just tender, about 4–6 minutes. Mash the butter and anchovies together in a small bowl. Toast the walnuts in a dry frying pan until golden and fragrant, then cool slightly before roughly chopping.

Toss the broccoli in the olive oil and vinegar and season. Toast or grill the bread, then spread with the anchovy butter while still warm. Arrange the broccoli over the bread then sprinkle with the the walnuts, capers and a little chopped parsley.

2. Butter beans

———

with tarragon & chives

[YOU WILL NEED]

2 Tbsp crème fraîche
150g [1 cup] crumbled feta
400g [scant 1⅔ cups] canned butter
   [lima] beans, drained
100g [3½oz] cherry tomatoes, halved
1 garlic clove, very finely chopped
a few tarragon leaves, roughly chopped
1 small bunch of chives, roughly chopped
½ lemon
4 slices of sourdough bread
1 Tbsp cold-pressed rapeseed oil
   or olive oil
cress, to serve
few basil leaves, to serve

Stir the crème fraîche and feta together in a large bowl. Add the butter beans, tomatoes, garlic, herbs and a squeeze of lemon juice then mix well.

Toast the bread and drizzle with a little oil. Top with the feta and bean mixture, a further drizzle of oil, some cress and a few basil leaves.

3. Prawn & avocado

——

with radishes & mustard

[YOU WILL NEED]

4 eggs
75g [⅓ cup] mayonnaise
1 Tbsp Dijon mustard
1 small bunch of chives, finely chopped
1 lemon, juice, plus wedges to serve
250g [9oz] Atlantic prawns [shrimp],
   shells on, defrosted and peeled
2 avocados, stoned, peeled and cubed
dash of Tabasco sauce, to taste
4 slices of rye or pumpernickel bread
8–10 radishes, sliced
dill, for sprinkling

Hard-boil the eggs in a pan of simmering water, about 10 minutes, depending on the size of the eggs. Place under cold running water and allow to cool before peeling and slicing.

Mix the mayonnaise with the mustard, chives, half the lemon juice and a good pinch of salt and pepper.

Combine the prawns, cubed avocado and a little lemon juice in a small bowl. Season to taste with the Tabasco. Spread the mustardy mayonnaise over the bread, then arrange the sliced egg over it. Top with the prawn and avocado mixture, the radish slices and sprinkle over a little dill. Serve with lemon wedges.

4. Peas & broad beans

——

with dill, mint & halloumi

[YOU WILL NEED]

150g [1⅓ cups] frozen or fresh broad
   [fava] beans
150g [1 cup] frozen or fresh peas
4 slices of rye or sourdough bread
1 garlic clove
cold-pressed rapeseed oil or olive oil,
   for drizzling
½ lemon, zest and juice
1 small bunch of dill, roughly chopped
1 small bunch of mint, roughly chopped
halloumi, shaved, for topping

Cook the broad beans in a pan of simmering water for 2 minutes (longer if using fresh beans), until just tender. Drain and rinse under cold running water, then pod the beans from their leathery skins (or leave on if short of time!).

Cover the frozen peas with boiling water and leave for a few minutes, then drain. If using fresh peas, cook in a pan of boiling water for 3–4 minutes.

Toast the bread and, while still hot, rub with the garlic clove and drizzle with a little oil.

Combine the beans and peas in a bowl with a pinch of sea salt and a squeeze of lemon juice. Mash a little with a fork, then stir through the lemon zest, herbs and a drizzle of oil. Spoon onto the toasted bread and top with some shaved halloumi.

This is one of my favourite recipes in the book. The fennel cuts through the oiliness of the mackerel really well and the creamy cheese adds freshness. I also love the contrast of soft fish and crunchy crispbread. This sandwich could really be a meal in itself with nothing more than a green salad and cold beer. A word of advice – do get your fishmonger to fillet and skin the mackerel for you or you'll go mad.

5. Fennel-crusted mackerel

——

on crispbread with potatoes & fresh cheese

[YOU WILL NEED]

5 baby potatoes, scrubbed
1 egg, beaten
1 Tbsp fennel seeds, bashed
50g [⅔ cup] dried breadcrumbs
4 mackerel fillets, pin-boned and skinned
2 tbsp cold-pressed rapeseed oil or
    olive oil
100g [scant ½ cup] fresh cheese
    (see page 108) or use ricotta
2 Tbsp mayonnaise
½ lemon, zest and juice
1 small bunch of parsley, roughly chopped
2 large round crispbreads, broken up

Begin by cooking the potatoes in a pan of boiling water until just tender, then drain and allow to cool slightly. Slice into thick rounds and set aside.

Meanwhile, beat the egg in a shallow bowl and mix the fennel and breadcrumbs together in another bowl. Dip the mackerel fillets in the egg, then dredge in the crumbs, coating completely.

Heat the oil in a large frying pan and fry the mackerel fillets until golden and crispy, about 4 minutes on each side.

Mix the cheese, mayonnaise, lemon zest and a squeeze of lemon juice together in a bowl. Stir through most of the parsley and season generously. Spread over the crispbreads, then top with the potato slices and fried fish. Sprinkle with a little more parsley and a few more drips of lemon juice before serving.

I first made a version of this terrine when I was studying to be a chef and it always stood out as something I would love to make for my friends and family back in Sweden. Using saffron, lemon and dill to season struck me as something they would like as these are so ubiquitous in our cooking. Although this has the "wow" factor and would make a great centrepiece for a weekend lunch, it is actually very easy to prepare. You don't have to be too precious when assembling it – the mackerel can be messily pieced together and it will still look great when sliced.

Smoked mackerel & trout terrine

——

with saffron potatoes

[YOU WILL NEED]

300g [10½oz] floury [mealy] potatoes, peeled and cut into chunks
2 generous pinches of saffron threads
600g [1¼lb] whole smoked mackerel (about 400g/14oz if you are using fillets only), pin-boned and skinned
50g [3½ Tbsp] butter, softened
1 Tbsp dill, finely chopped, plus extra to garnish
1 lemon, zest and juice
4–5 hot smoked trout fillets

[SERVES 8]

Put the potatoes in a large pan of salted water, along with a pinch of saffron, and bring to a simmer. Line a large terrine mould, or 900-g [2-lb] loaf tin, with a double layer of clingfilm. You may find it easier to do this if you brush the tin with a little water first. There should be plenty of overhang.

If using whole mackerel, separate these into fillets and use to line the bottom and up the sides of the mould, packing them tightly. The fillets will easily mould to each other and you can use any smaller pieces to patch up any gaps. Reserve a few fillets for the top.

Once the potatoes are cooked through, drain them and return to the hot pan for a minute to get rid of any excess moisture and fluff them up a little. Add the butter, remaining saffron, dill, lemon zest and a little lemon juice to taste. Mix together so the potatoes break up a bit. Season with salt and pepper.

Pack half the potatoes into the tin, then layer with the trout and then the remaining potatoes. Finish with the rest of the mackerel. Tightly wrap with the overhanging clingfilm and a layer of foil, then weigh down with some cans of food. Refrigerate for at least 4 hours, ideally overnight.

When ready to serve, carefully unwrap the top of the terrine and invert onto a plate to release from the tin. Remove the clingfilm, cut into generous slices and sprinkle with more dill to garnish. Serve with salad and horseradish mayo, if you like.

If you ever find yourself in a pizzeria anywhere in Sweden, you will likely encounter a side dish of punchy cabbage slaw to go with your order, known as pizzasallad. It is basically a simple slaw with a sharp vinegary dressing that's totally addictive. Pizza doesn't really taste the same without it but you can also serve it as a side salad with meat, fish or as part of a picnic. I have added some seeds for extra crunch.

Pizzasallad

—

[*Crunchy cabbage slaw with seeds*]

[YOU WILL NEED]

500g [1lb 2 oz] white cabbage
1 grilled red [bell] pepper in oil, sliced
1 small red onion, finely sliced
3 Tbsp cold-pressed rapeseed oil or
    olive oil
1 Tbsp white wine vinegar
½ tsp dried oregano
pinch of chilli [red pepper] flakes
1 tsp poppy seeds
1 tsp sunflower seeds

[SERVES 4]

Begin by very finely shredding the cabbage, ideally using a slicing attachment in a food processor. Place the shredded cabbage in a large sieve and sprinkle over about 2 teaspoons sea salt. Leave for 20–30 minutes, then drain away any liquid and shake off any excess salt.

Place the cabbage in a large bowl and add the red pepper and onion. Whisk the oil and vinegar together with the oregano, chilli flakes and plenty of black pepper. Pour the dressing over the salad and add the seeds, tossing to distribute. Serve as a slaw or with pizza.

This is a really simple side dish that makes a perfect accompaniment to lamb in the spring. If you want to make it the star of the show for lunch or a light supper, serve with some ham or cold chicken, a dollop of mustard and a chunk of rye bread.

Braised lettuce

———

with peas & shallots

[YOU WILL NEED]

1 Tbsp olive oil
2 banana shallots
4 little gem lettuces
100ml [scant ½ cup] hot vegetable or
    chicken stock [broth]
1 Tbsp butter
150g [1 cup] fresh or frozen peas
few tarragon leaves, roughly chopped
1 small bunch of parsley, roughly chopped

[SERVES 4 AS A SIDE OR
2 FOR LUNCH]

Heat the olive oil in a large saucepan, add the shallots and fry over a gentle heat until softened, about 5 minutes.

Meanwhile, trim the roots of the lettuces a little, while still keeping them intact. Halve them lengthways.

Place the lettuces cut-side down in the pan and pour over the hot stock. Increase the heat and let bubble away until the stock has reduced by half; this should only take a few minutes. Add the butter and peas and cover with a lid. Cook for another minute or two, then uncover, sprinkle with the herbs and serve immediately.

The Swedes eat a lot of game and hunting is a much more commonplace pastime than in many other parts of Europe, particularly in the autumn and winter months. Wild boar, elk and moose are among the most common game meats. As moose is pretty tricky to track down, I have used venison here, which is widely available, as well as some game birds. Wild game is low in fat and high in protein and so really good for you, but many find cooking with it an intimidating prospect. Here is an introduction to game that may prove more palatable than a joint. Serve the terrine with these vanilla-poached cherry tomatoes, a great alternative to a chutney, inspired by a dish I tried in Bornholm, off the Danish coast.

Game terrine

—

served with vanilla-poached cherry tomatoes

[YOU WILL NEED]

100g [scant 1 cup] prunes, stoned
4 Tbsp brandy
2 Tbsp olive oil, plus a little extra
    for greasing
200g [7oz] diced venison (deer)
150g [5¼oz] duck breasts, skin removed
    and cut into 1-cm [½-in] strips
100g [3½oz] fresh bread slices
    (white or brown)
2 sage sprigs, leaves picked
1 tsp ground ginger
2 allspice berries
6 juniper berries
200g [7oz] chicken or duck livers
300g [10½oz] sausage meat
100ml [scant ½ cup] red wine
1 egg
150g [5¼oz] pancetta rashers [slices]
toasted bread, to serve

For the cherry tomatoes
30g [2½ Tbsp] sugar
1 vanilla pod [bean], split in half lengthways
½ lemon, juice
330g [2 cups] cherry tomatoes

[SERVES 8]

Soak the prunes in brandy overnight. You can make the cherry tomatoes in advance – place 100ml [7 Tbsp] water in a pan with the sugar, vanilla and 1 tablespoon lemon juice. Bring to a simmer and let the sugar dissolve, then add the tomatoes and poach for 10 minutes. Remove the tomatoes with a slotted spoon and set aside while the liquid reduces until syrupy. Pour over the tomatoes and cool before refrigerating.

The next morning, heat the oil in a frying pan and fry the venison and duck in batches for a few minutes on each side until browned, then add to a bowl with the soaked prunes. Preheat the oven to 175°C/350°F and boil the kettle. Blitz the bread, sage and spices in a food processor until crumb-like. Add the liver, sausage meat, red wine and egg and continue to mix until everything is completely incorporated.

Oil a 900-g [2-lb] loaf tin and line with a single layer of the pancetta. You may need to flatten them to get them to stretch – there should be some overhang. Fill the tin with half of the sausage-meat mixture, flattening slightly. Arrange the venison, duck and prunes on top, then add the remaining sausage-meat mixture and fold up the pancetta ends. Top with any remaining pancetta, then cover tightly with foil. Place in a roasting tray and pour in hot water to about halfway up the tray. Bake for 1½ hours, then test by piercing with a knife – the juices should run clear. Drain off any liquid.

Weigh the terrine down with a plate and few cans of food on top. Cool completely before refrigerating for a few hours. To serve, run a knife along the edges then place a dish over the top. Tip upside down and slide out of the tin. Slice thickly and serve with the poached tomatoes and toasted bread.

I have wonderful memories of artichokes. In Sweden, they come into season in the late summer (everything is slightly delayed up north) and I can remember sitting on our veranda, tugging out the leaves, dipping them in melted butter and then pulling off the softest flesh with my teeth. There is something wonderful about this ritual that automatically makes you slow down. It is a sociable, messy and time-consuming dish and one to be revered. For a lighter option, I would suggest dipping the artichokes in a quick dip made from Greek yogurt, a scant spoonful of mayonnaise, garlic and herbs.

Steamed artichokes

——

with whipped brown butter

[YOU WILL NEED]
100g [7 Tbsp] butter, softened
½ lemon
2 medium artichokes

[SERVES 2]

Start by browning the butter. Spoon half the butter into a frying pan and melt over a medium-high heat. Continue to cook until it starts to go brown and smell nutty. You will see little golden flecks appear – watch carefully so these don't burn. Remove from the heat.

Place the remaining butter in a medium bowl and pour over the contents of the frying pan, scraping any bits from the bottom into the bowl. Sprinkle with a little sea salt and a few gratings of lemon zest, then allow to cool completely until the butter starts to solidify.

Using electric beaters, whisk the butter until creamy, pale and speckled, then refrigerate while you steam the artichokes.

To prepare the artichokes, first remove a layer of the tough outer leaves, then cut off the top third of the vegetable. Trim the tips of the leaves around the sides with a pair of scissors and rub the top and any exposed flesh with the lemon half. Trim the stem down so you can sit the artichokes upright.

Put the lemon half in a large, lidded saucepan and pour in about 2.5cm [1in] water. Place a metal steaming basket inside the pan and bring to a gentle simmer. Sit the artichokes in the basket and clamp on the lid. The artichokes will take anything from 30–45 minutes to steam completely, depending on their size. You will know they are cooked when you can pull a leaf out with no resistance. Remove the butter from the fridge and re-whip if necessary.

Serve the artichokes with the whipped brown butter on the side.

A CELEBRATION OF BEETROOT

Four vibrant recipes

---

[1]   Quick pickled beetroot with chillies & anise
[2]   Beetroot tarte Tatin with salsa verde
[3]   Creamy beetroot linguine with cannellini beans & walnuts
[4]   Beetroot & rosemary fritters with blue-cheese cream

Beetroot features in many Scandinavian cookbooks, often pickled or as a way to add colour and flavour to *gravadlax*. And, while it is a popular vegetable, it is perhaps not quite as ubiquitous as these books would have us believe. This isn't to say that it doesn't make an appearance from time to time on our tables, but more often than not they are served with little ceremony, enjoyed for their sweet, earthy flavour by simply roasting or serving boiled with a little fresh cheese or butter.

A particular, traditional favourite is cooked beetroot, chopped into cubes with apple and served in a salad with plenty of mayonnaise as a creamy, almost fluorescent pink sandwich topper or side dish. Here are some other ideas for making the most of this misaligned root. All of these recipes use fresh beetroot – not the brined or cooked versions, which while convenient, are a bit too astringent for my taste.

"Trampa inte rödbetor i mossen"
["Don't trample beetroot into the bog", i.e. don't sweat the small stuff!]
SWEDISH SAYING

This is a spicier take on the traditional pickled beetroot. It is ready the next day so does not need a long period of pickling for the flavours to kick in. Serve with ham, cheese, in salads – however you please.

1. Quick pickled beetroot

———

with chillies & anise

[YOU WILL NEED]

800g [1¾lb] small beetroot [beet]
500ml [generous 2 cups] white
   wine vinegar
150g [generous ¾ cup] golden caster
   [unrefined granulated] sugar
1 tsp dried chillies
2 bay leaves
1 tsp white peppercorns
1 star anise
1 tsp juniper berries

[MAKES 1 JAR]

Wash, trim and scrub the beetroot carefully, making sure they don't bleed too much. Bring a large pan of water to the boil and add the beetroot, cooking until just tender, about 40 minutes. Allow to cool a little, then cut into wedges.

Heat the vinegar, sugar, chillies, bay leaves and spices in a small saucepan over a low heat until the sugar has dissolved.

Transfer the beetroot to a sterilized jar and pour over the liquid. Seal and allow to cool completely before refrigerating. The beetroot is ready the next day and can be stored in a cool place for up to 1 month.

This is a really special way to celebrate beetroot – it looks stunning, it's easy and it works as a starter or a main course. You can use a combination of your favourite herbs for the salsa verde to finish off the tart.

2. Beetroot tarte Tatin

———

with salsa verde

[YOU WILL NEED]

For the tarte Tatin
400g [14oz] small fresh beetroot
    [beet], scrubbed
½ block puff pastry [250g/9oz]
3 tbsp pure maple syrup
1 tbsp sherry vinegar
2 sprigs of thyme, leaves picked
1 egg, beaten

For the salsa verde
3 tbsp green olives, stoned
½ garlic clove
3 Tbsp olive oil
1 Tbsp sherry vinegar
squeeze of lemon juice
1 large bunch leafy mixed herbs
    (e.g. mint, parsley, basil and thyme)

To serve
rocket [arugula]
feta, crumbled

[SERVES 2 FOR LUNCH,
OR 4 AS A STARTER]

For the tarte Tatin, bring a saucepan of water to the boil then pop in beetroot. Cook for 30 minutes, or until soft when pierced with a knife. Drain and cool before cutting into 1-cm [⅜-in] thick slices.

Preheat the oven to 200°C/400°F. Roll the puff pastry out to about 3mm [⅛in] thick. Cut out a circle using an ovenproof frying pan (about 20cm/8in in diameter) as your guide. Refrigerate.

Place the frying pan on a high heat and add the maple syrup with a pinch of sea salt. Bubble away for a couple of minutes. Add the sherry vinegar and thyme, swirling around the pan for about 30 seconds before removing from the heat. Arrange the beetroot slices in the pan, overlapping a little.

Working quickly, drape the pastry over the beetroot, tucking it in around the edges. Brush the egg all over the pastry and bake for 25–30 minutes until puffed up and golden.

Meanwhile, make the salsa verde by blitzing all of the ingredients in a blender, adding a splash of water if too thick. Season with salt and pepper.

Turn the tarte out onto a plate using a palette knife to help you. Scatter some rocket and feta over the tart, then spoon over the salsa verde.

Beetroot and pasta are perhaps not the most obvious bedfellows, but with a little bit of vinegar and crème fraîche to counterbalance the beetroot's sweetness, this is a combo that really works. It is also a great way to introduce kids to this knobbly root vegetable – who can resist bright pink spaghetti?

3. Creamy beetroot linguine

——

with cannellini beans & walnuts

[YOU WILL NEED]

4 medium beetroot [beet], scrubbed and
    cut into wedges
4 garlic cloves, unpeeled
2 Tbsp olive oil
few thyme sprigs, leaves picked
400g [2¾ cups] canned cannellini beans,
    drained
1 Tbsp red wine vinegar
3 Tbsp crème fraîche
400g [14oz] wholemeal [whole-wheat]
    linguine
feta, crumbled, to serve
few dill sprigs, roughly chopped, to serve
toasted walnuts, to serve

[SERVES 4]

Preheat the oven to 200°C/400°F. Place the beetroot [beet] wedges and garlic in a roasting tray and drizzle with the oil. Season with salt and pepper and sprinkle over the thyme leaves. Roast for 30–40 minutes, until tender and beginning to caramelize.

Remove from the oven, and trim any tough, darker bits off the beetroot. Put in a food processor or, if using a stick blender, a deep jug. Squeeze the garlic from their skins and add to the beetroot.

Tip in the cannellini beans, vinegar, crème fraîche and 100ml [7 Tbsp] water and blitz until you have a smooth paste – add more water if it seems very thick.

Cook the linguine according to the packet instructions and drain. Return to the still-warm pan and stir through the beetroot sauce. Serve topped with a little crumbled feta, some dill and toasted walnuts for crunch.

This is a quick veggie supper that tastes both earthy and sweet. I like strong blue cheese here to balance out the flavours, but you could just as easily use feta or goat's cheese if you prefer something milder. Serve with some leaves or, alternatively, top with a fried egg and some slices of ham.

4. Beetroot & rosemary fritters

―――

with blue-cheese cream

[YOU WILL NEED]

For the fritters
500g [1lb 2oz] beetroot [beet], peeled
1 onion
2 medium potatoes, cooked until soft
2 Tbsp plain [all-purpose] flour
1 egg
1 rosemary sprig, leaves picked and
    finely chopped
1 small bunch of parsley, finely chopped
2 Tbsp cold-pressed rapeseed oil or
    olive oil

For the cream
100g [3½oz] creamy blue cheese,
    such as Roquefort
100g [½ cup] half-fat crème fraîche
2 Tbsp mayonnaise
1 tsp balsamic vinegar

To serve
rocket [arugula] and watercress salad

[SERVES 4]

Begin by coarsely grating the beetroot and onion into a large bowl. This may well be a messy process so don't wear your favourite shirt. Roughly mash the potatoes with a fork before mixing together with the beetroot.

Add the flour, egg, rosemary, parsley and plenty of seasoning and mix well. Form the mixture into 7–8 thick patties, about 8cm [3¼in] in diameter and set aside.

To make the cream, mash the blue cheese in a bowl, then whisk in the crème fraîche to loosen. Add the mayonnaise and balsamic vinegar, then season to taste.

Heat the oil in a large frying pan and fry the fritters over a low-medium heat for about 8–10 minutes on each side, until crisp and cooked through.

Serve immediately with the blue cheese cream and a rocket and watercress salad.

Roasted Jerusalem artichokes

with goat's curd, tarragon & flaked almonds

[YOU WILL NEED]

700g [1½lb] Jerusalem artichokes,
  scrubbed, larger ones halved
4 Tbsp olive oil
4 garlic cloves
few rosemary sprigs
5 tarragon leaves, finely chopped
½ lemon, juice
1 tsp wholegrain mustard
goat's curd or soft goat's cheese, crumbled
2 Tbsp flaked [slivered] almonds, toasted

[SERVES 4]

Preheat the oven to 180°C/350°F. Toss the Jerusalem artichokes in half of the olive oil on a roasting tray with the garlic, rosemary and plenty of seasoning. Roast for 35–40 minutes, until soft and golden.

Meanwhile, mix the tarragon with the remaining olive oil, a squeeze of lemon juice, mustard and some salt and pepper. Drizzle over the roasted Jerusalem artichokes and serve dolloped with crumbled goat's cheese and sprinkled with toasted flaked almonds.

Apple & parsnip soup

with juniper & dill

[YOU WILL NEED]

2 Tbsp olive oil
2 shallots, chopped
2 celery sticks, chopped
3 tart apples
2 large parsnips (about 300g/10½oz)
2 garlic cloves, very finely chopped
1 thumb of fresh ginger, peeled and grated
250ml [1 cup] dry apple cider
1.2 litres [5 cups] chicken stock [broth]
1 tsp juniper berries
4 whole cardamom pods
1 small cinnamon stick
150ml [⅔ cup] single [light] cream
1 small bunch of dill or parsley, chopped

[SERVES 4]

Heat the olive oil in a large pan, add the shallots and fry for a minute or two until starting to soften. Add the celery and cook over a low heat for 5 minutes. Peel and roughly chop the apples and parsnips, then add to the pan with the garlic and ginger and cook for a further 5 minutes before pouring in the cider. Let bubble for a minute before adding the stock.

Put the spices in a scrap of muslin [cheesecloth], fold up the corners and tie together; alternatively, place in an enclosed tea infuser. Add to the soup, bring to the boil, then reduce the heat and simmer for 30 minutes until the apples and parsnips are soft.

Remove and discard the spices and purée the soup with a stick blender or in a food processor until smooth. Bring to a simmer again and stir through the cream, if using. Taste to season and scatter over the dill or parsley.

HUVUDRÄTTER
[main meals]

Growing up, dinner was always strictly observed; it was a proper, sit-down affair at a set time with the whole family – no exceptions. I remember being told off for not finishing phone calls quickly enough when it was time to eat – who would call in the middle of dinner?!

Meals were simple but always made from scratch, combining protein (with fish served as often as meat), whole grains and plenty of vegetables. Winter tended to be a time for comfort foods, for hunkering down, whereas during our summers spent in the Stockholm archipelago, meals were more relaxed, often eaten outside in the light summer evenings. Swedes are obsessed with cooking outdoors for the short amount of time that it is possible, so BBQs were a weekday affair as well as for special occasions.

If I was particularly lucky, there might be dinner in front of the TV – an exciting, rare treat that always felt pretty special, even indulgent. This was most often reserved for the start of the weekend, what the Swedes call *fredagsmys* or "cosy Friday".

While all this might sound a bit prescriptive, and perhaps it was, it did instil in me the importance of the evening meal, of sitting down to a balanced dish that was home cooked and shared. The prospect of what was for dinner always felt exciting to me, not least because I had a mother who wasn't afraid of experimenting with different flavours and recipes.

I've always felt that there is a freshness and boldness to Swedish cooking that is frequently overlooked. The emphasis is on what is seasonal, fresh and good for you but, above all, delicious. The resulting dishes are rich and varied in flavour, drawing on cuisines from around the world and wonderfully full of zest.

The recipes in this section reflect this, and range from meals that work for busy weekdays and others for when you have time to spend. "*Ingen ko på isen*", as we would say – "no cow on the ice", i.e. no rush. Think of cosy Friday nights in, winter lunches with friends, or balmy summer evenings that stretch out until even the Swedish sun sets.

"*Ingen ko på isen*"
["No cow on the ice", i.e. no need to worry]
SWEDISH SAYING

This may sound like an unusual combination, but braising in almond milk helps to keep the pork moist and tender. It also makes a delicious gravy once the dish is finsished. Be sure to heat the almond milk before adding to the pork, as this helps to avoid splitting, and to brush off any excess salt before serving.

Almond milk-braised pork belly

——

with peas, watercress & samphire

[YOU WILL NEED]

1.2kg [2¾lb] rolled and tied pork belly, skin scored
1 Tbsp olive oil, plus a little extra
750ml [3 cups] unsweetened almond milk
1 small bunch of sage
1 tsp fennel seeds
2 bay leaves
pinch of chilli [red pepper] flakes
150g [scant 1 cup] fresh or frozen peas
2 shallots, sliced
1 garlic clove, finely chopped
100g [3½oz] samphire
1 small bag of watercress (about 100g/3½oz)

[SERVES 4]

Preheat the oven to 240°C/475°F. Rub the pork with the olive oil and place in a snug roasting tray. Sprinkle the skin with plenty of sea salt and roast for 25 minutes until the skin starts to blister.

Reduce the oven temperature to 180°C/350°F and continue to cook for 1 hour. Pour the almond milk into a saucepan with the sage, fennel seeds, bay leaves and chilli flakes and heat very gently. Once the pork has been cooking for its hour, spoon out any fat from the tray, then tip in the hot almond milk, pouring all around the meat but not on top of it. Return to the oven for a further hour – it's ready when the meat pulls away easily.

Finally, raise the oven temperature to its highest setting and cook for about 10 minutes until the pork skin has crackled all over. Remove from the tray (reserving the almondy juices) and allow to rest on a carving board, covered with foil.

Cook the peas in a small pan of boiling water for a few minutes (longer if using fresh peas), then drain. In a large frying pan, heat a little oil and gently fry the shallots until softened, about 5 minutes. Add the garlic and samphire and sauté, stirring frequently, until the samphire is just tender, about 4–5 minutes. Add the peas and watercress and cook until the watercress has just wilted.

Strain the almond milk into a jug to remove the herbs and spices, then pour back into the tray. Set this over a low heat and simmer until saucy. The milk may split slightly, but don't worry too much about this as it will still taste delicious.

Brush any excess salt off the pork and carve into thick slices. Serve with the vegetables and almond milk gravy.

Pearl barley can run the risk of giving a dish a slightly woolly taste if you aren't careful. However, in a risotto, I find it takes on other flavours really well, while adding both bite and depth. I have topped this one with a quick cured salmon, for those who don't have the patience to go through a full curing process. It is also great for smaller amounts of fish, as a whole cured salmon can be tricky to get through if you aren't throwing a big party.

Creamy pearl barley risotto

——

with smoked garlic, asparagus & quick cured salmon

[YOU WILL NEED]

1 Tbsp olive oil
1 onion, finely chopped
300g [scant 1⅔ cups] pearl barley
1.5 litres [6½ cups] vegetable or chicken
    stock [broth]
200g [7oz] sushi-grade salmon fillet,
    very thinly sliced
2 tsp sugar
ground white pepper
1 lime, zest and juice
300ml [1¼ cups] half-fat crème fraîche
3 smoked garlic cloves (or regular garlic
    if unavailable), peeled and quartered
100g [3½oz] asparagus tips, cut
    into chunks
1 small bunch of dill
Parmesan cheese, shaved, to serve

[SERVES 4]

Heat the olive oil in a large saucepan, add the onion and cook until soft over a low heat without colouring, about 10 minutes. Stir in the pearl barley and pour in the stock. Simmer for 30–45 minutes (depending on your barley), stirring occasionally until most of the liquid has been absorbed and the grains are soft with just a little bite.

While the pearl barley is cooking, arrange the salmon slices on a large plate, touching but overlapping as little as possible. Mix the sugar, 2 teaspoons sea salt, a good grind of white pepper and the lime zest and juice together in a small bowl. Sprinkle over the salmon then cover with clingfilm and chill for at least 30 minutes, turning halfway through.

Pour the crème fraîche into a small saucepan with the garlic. Bring to the boil, then reduce the heat and simmer for 10 minutes. Turn off the heat and leave to infuse for 15 minutes.

Blitz the garlic cream in a blender until smooth, then pour into the barley. Heat, stirring constantly, until thick and oozy.

Steam the asparagus until just tender, then stir all but a few tips through the pearl barley, along with most of the dill, reserving a few stalks for garnishing. Spoon the risotto into bowls, top with a few slices of salmon and the remaining asparagus tips. Sprinkle over a little dill and some Parmesan.

*NOTE quick cured salmon ideas

You could also serve this salmon on little pieces of rye or crispbread with lemon and dill for a pre-dinner nibble, stirred through creamy pasta, or given a starring role in a peppery rocket salad with a mustardy vinaigrette.

This is a weekend dish for when there is time to cook for friends and family. This is a slow, rich stew for a long winter lunch. The good news is, once it is in the oven it requires very little work – so you can put your feet up! My husband particularly likes this with buttered tagliatelle, omitting the pears in favour of a little wilted spinach.

Slow-braised pork cheeks

—

with pear, sage & candied walnuts

[YOU WILL NEED]

3 Tbsp plain [all-purpose] flour
1 tsp paprika
1kg [2¼lb] pork cheeks, fat trimmed and cut in half through their middles if very thick
3 Tbsp cold-pressed rapeseed oil or olive oil
1 onion, roughly chopped
3 celery sticks, roughly chopped
2 carrots, roughly chopped
2 garlic cloves, finely chopped
2 Tbsp tomato purée [paste]
200ml [scant 1 cup] red wine
500ml [generous 2 cups] beef stock [broth]
1 sprig each of thyme, rosemary and parsley
1 small bunch of sage, roughly chopped, plus reserved 1 sprig
2 bay leaves
75g [½ cup] walnut halves
1 Tbsp caster sugar
2 Tbsp butter
1 Tbsp soft brown sugar
3 pears, halved and cut into quarters

[SERVES 4-6]

Preheat the oven to 160°C/325°F. Mix the flour with the paprika and plenty of salt and pepper in a shallow bowl. Coat the pork cheeks in the flour mixture.

Heat 2 tablespoons of the oil in a large, ovenproof casserole dish and fry the cheeks in batches until browned all over. Set aside, then add the remaining oil to the pan and tip in the onion. Cook, colouring as little as possible, for 5 minutes. Add the celery and carrots and fry for a further 5 minutes, stirring frequently. Add the garlic and tomato purée and cook for a minute or two before returning the cheeks to the pan. Pour in the red wine and simmer for a few minutes, scraping the bottom of the pan.

Cover the pork and vegetables with the stock, then add the thyme, rosemary, parsley, sage sprig and bay leaves, all tied together with string. Cover with a lid and transfer to the oven, cooking for about 3 hours, or until the pork cheeks are tender come apart easily.

Meanwhile, toss the walnuts with a spoonful of water and the caster sugar. Tip onto a baking sheet and place at the bottom of the oven for 10–15 minutes, stirring halfway through, until golden and caramelized.

When the pork is almost ready, melt the butter in a large frying pan. Stir in the brown sugar and add the pears, cooking for about 5 minutes until golden and softened. Remove from the pan and sprinkle in the chopped sage leaves. Fry in the caramel butter briefly until crisp then scatter over the pears.

Remove the herbs from the casserole dish and sprinkle the pork with the walnuts. Serve with the sage pears.

I have oven-baked these as I find that most appropriate for a lighter everyday meal. However, should you feel like indulging, there is nothing to stop you from pan-frying these in oil and butter, basting frequently, for that authentic, indulgent schnitzel taste.

Crispbread schnitzel

——

with crunchy buttermilk slaw

[YOU WILL NEED]

For the slaw
½ head of white cabbage, thinly sliced
½ cucumber, halved lengthways
2 celery sticks, finely sliced
75ml [5 Tbsp] buttermilk
1 Tbsp olive oil
2 Tbsp mayonnaise
1 tsp Dijon mustard
2 tsp apple cider vinegar
1 tsp caraway seeds
pinch of sugar
1 small bunch of parsley, finely chopped

For the schnitzels
1 egg, beaten
2 Tbsp plain [all-purpose] flour
2 crispbreads, blitzed or smashed into
   a fine crumb
1 lemon, zest, plus juice to serve
1 small bunch of chives, finely chopped
2 veal or pork escalopes [scallops]
oil spray (best quality available)

[SERVES 2]

To make the slaw, place the cabbage in a large sieve and sprinkle all over with sea salt. Leave for 10 minutes, then shake or brush off any excess salt. Scoop the seeds out of the cucumber and thinly slice. Place in a large bowl with the celery and cabbage. Whisk the buttermilk, olive oil, mayonnaise, Dijon mustard, vinegar and caraway seeds together in a bowl. Season with the sugar, salt and pepper and the chopped parsley. Toss the dressing into the slaw.

Preheat the oven to 200°C/400°F and lightly grease a baking sheet with a little oil. Assemble 3 shallow bowls and place the beaten egg in one and the flour in the second. In the third bowl, mix the crispbread crumbs together with the lemon zest, chives and some seasoning. Flatten the escalopes under some baking parchment by bashing with a rolling pin, taking care not to tear. They should be about 5mm [¼in] thick.

Coat the escalopes with the flour, dip in the egg, then coat with the crumbs. Place on the prepared baking sheet and spritz with a little oil spray. Bake for 20 minutes, flipping halfway through and re-spraying with oil. They should be golden and cooked through. Serve squeezed with lemon juice and with the slaw.

Baked chicken thighs

with white wine & gooseberries

[YOU WILL NEED]

2 onions, sliced
600g [1¼lb] bone-in chicken thighs,
   skin on
300g [scant 2⅔ cups] gooseberries
   (rhubarb cut into 2-cm [¾-in] chunks
   also works well)
1 Tbsp olive oil
½ thumb of fresh ginger, peeled
   and grated
2 garlic cloves, finely chopped
200ml [scant 1 cup] white wine
few thyme sprigs, leaves picked

[SERVES 4]

Preheat the oven to 200°C/400°F. Place the onion slices on the bottom of a roasting tray. Arrange the chicken thighs on top and scatter the gooseberries all around. Drizzle the chicken with the olive oil and season with salt and pepper.

Mix the ginger and garlic together in a jug with the wine. Whisk to combine, then pour all around the chicken. Sprinkle the thyme leaves over the chicken and bake for 25–30 minutes, until the chicken is crispy and cooked through and the wine has reduced a little to a sauce. Serve with a crunchy salad.

Slow-cooked pork

with sweet mustard & root vegetables

[YOU WILL NEED]

4 large parsnips, halved
1 swede [rutabaga], cut into large chunks
3 celery sticks, cut into chunks
3 carrots, cut into chunks
1 small bunch of thyme
2 Tbsp sweet mustard (Swedish or
   American), plus extra to serve
2 garlic cloves
1 small bunch of sage, finely chopped
1 small bunch of parsley, finely chopped
1.5–2kg [3¼–4lb] pork shoulder
200ml [scant 1 cup] cider
300ml [1¼ cups] chicken stock [broth]

[SERVES 4-6]

Preheat the oven to 220°C/425°F. Arrange the vegetables and thyme in a large roasting tray. Mix the mustard, garlic, sage, parsley and lots of salt and pepper in a small bowl. Score the pork skin with a sharp knife and brush with the mustard mixture. Place on top of the vegetables, then pour in the cider and stock.

Roast for 30 minutes. Reduce the oven temperature to 140°C/275°F and cover the whole tray with foil. Continue to roast for 4 hours, or until the pork comes apart easily. Baste with the liquid at least once an hour. Serve with more mustard and the accompanying vegetables.

This recipe is ideal for a party as it can be scaled up to serve lots of people. Twice- or double-marinated pork is a trendy way to cook pork tenderloin in Sweden and the effort involved gives you licence to show off a bit. This is probably the longest-to-prepare recipe in this book – three days in total! However, the overall elbow grease over those three days is pretty minimal. The second marinade acts as a dressing for the meat, adding further flavour.

Twice-marinated pork tenderloin

—

with chimichurri

[YOU WILL NEED]
750g [1lb 10oz] pork tenderloins
cold-pressed rapeseed oil or olive oil,
    for frying
1 lime, thinly sliced, to serve
1 small bunch of mint, leaves picked, to serve

For the first marinade
1 Tbsp white wine vinegar
½ Tbsp balsamic vinegar
2 tsp dark muscovado [brown] sugar
½ tsp smoked paprika
¼ tsp chilli powder
2 Tbsp tomato purée [paste]

For the second marinade
2 Tbsp dark muscovado [brown] sugar
½ Tbsp balsamic vinegar
50ml [½ Tbsp] lime juice
100ml [7 Tbsp] rapeseed oil or olive oil
1 red chilli, finely chopped
2 garlic cloves, thinly sliced

For the chimichurri
2 Tbsp red wine vinegar
1 garlic clove, finely chopped
1 small shallot, finely chopped
1 green chilli, finely chopped
1 small bunch of parsley, finely chopped
1 small bunch coriander [cilantro],
    finely chopped
75ml [5 Tbsp] extra virgin olive oil

[SERVES 4-6]

Whisk together all the ingredients for the first marinade. Trim any fat and sinew off the pork tenderloin, then place the pork in a large, sealable freezer bag and pour in the marinade, making sure the meat is well covered. Seal securely, place on a plate and refrigerate overnight.

The next day, preheat the oven to 150°C/300°F. Heat a little oil in a large frying pan and brown the tenderloins all over, taking care not to burn. Transfer to a roasting dish, season and bake for about 25–30 minutes until the inner temperature of the meat reaches 70°C/158°F. Allow to cool completely.

Make the second marinade by whisking together the sugar, vinegar, lime juice and oil. Add the chilli and garlic and season. Slice the meat into rounds about 1cm [½in] thick. Place the slices in another freezer bag and pour over the marinade. Seal and chill overnight.

The next day, remove the meat from the fridge, so that it isn't fridge-cold when served.

Make the chimichurri by whisking together all the ingredients along with the coriander in a small bowl with a little seasoning. To serve, arrange the tenderloin on a platter with the lime slices. Drizzle over any leftover second marinade and scatter with mint leaves. Serve with the chimichurri alongside.

OK, LET'S TALK
ABOUT MEATBALLS...

Three recipes to challenge your misconceptions

[1] Pork, pumpkin & sage meatballs with lemon cream
[2] Pollock dumplings with coconut & chilli noodle soup
[3] Lamb meatballs with lentils & cumin

This is a sensitive issue for me, one that fills me in equal parts with pride and prejudice. On the one hand, there are all the associations with the hurdy-gurdy chef from *Sesame Street*, the Abba-esque accents and of course the canteen of a certain furniture megastore. On the other, there's what I know: my grandmother's gorgeous, traditional, buttery speciality – half beef and half pork, laced with breadcrumbs, stock and lots of pepper; served frequently and much loved. We don't normally have them with jam and mash, they just form part of a buffet (yes, yes, a *smörgåsbord*) when there's lots of family and friends to feed. No occasion seems complete without them, but, as a firm kids' favourite, they are equally served at family dinner tables every day. However, there is no need to resign them to rigid tradition, to salt, to butter and to the frying pan. They can be made much healthier by baking them in the oven and serving with lots of vegetables. My cumin-scented lamb meatballs are bulked out with lentils, which keeps them wonderfully moist. I also love to make a pork and pumpkin version, and the fish ball is also very popular – mine are Thai scented and served in a chilli noodle soup.

"Man får väl dom köttbullar man förtjänar"
["I guess you get the meatballs you deserve"]

DESIRÉE IN THE FILM *GRABBEN I GRAVEN BREDVID*
[*THE GUY IN THE GRAVE NEXT DOOR*, 2002]

I like to serve these with cavolo nero, some Tenderstem broccoli, or other leafy veg. Alternatively, stir the lemon cream through some wholemeal tagliatelle and top with the meatballs.

1. Pork, pumpkin & sage meatballs

—

with lemon cream

[YOU WILL NEED]
For the meatballs
olive oil, for greasing
500g [scant 2¼ cups] pork mince
    [ground pork]
¼ medium pumpkin or butternut
    squash (about 200g/7oz), peeled
    and coarsely grated
1 apple, coarsely grated
1 red onion, coarsely grated
1 Tbsp finely chopped sage
2 garlic cloves, crushed
2 lemons, zest
75g [generous ½ cup] plain
    [all-purpose] flour
1 handful of toasted pine nuts, to serve

For the lemon cream
1 lemon, zest and juice
100g [7 Tbsp] crème fraîche
½ garlic clove, crushed
1 Tbsp honey

[SERVES 4]

Preheat the oven to 200°C/400°F and generously grease a roasting tray with oil. In a large bowl, combine the pork, pumpkin, apple and red onion. Stir through the sage, garlic and the zest of 1 lemon. Finally, sift over the flour and season generously. Stir, adding a little more flour if it seems very gloopy – although be aware that this should be quite a wet mixture to prevent the meatballs from drying out.

Roll into walnut-sized meatballs, about 5cm [2in] in diameter and place on the prepared roasting tray. Bake for about 20–25 minutes, shaking the tray occasionally, until all the meatballs are nicely browned and cooked through.

Meanwhile, for the lemon cream, mix the lemon juice and zest, crème fraîche, garlic and honey together in a bowl. Sprinkle the meatballs with the remaining lemon zest and the pine nuts, then serve with the lemon cream.

One of my earliest memories is of eating fiskbullar *(effectively "fish balls") for lunch at* dagis *(day care) in Sweden. I must have been 3 or 4 years old, they came canned in a dill sauce, heated up and served with potatoes, and I loved them. That early meal intertwined with fuzzy memories of naps and playgrounds must have had an impact because I still think of them fondly. And really, the idea of fish balls is not a bad one at all. Here, these soft dumplings are lightly spiced in a Thai-inspired noodle broth that makes for a delicious light supper.*

2. Pollock dumplings

——

with coconut & chilli noodle soup

[YOU WILL NEED]

For the dumplings
500g [1lb 2oz] pollock (or haddock),
   skinless and pin-boned
2 Tbsp soy sauce
1 Tbsp fish sauce
½ lime, zest and juice
1 red chilli, finely chopped
½ thumb of fresh ginger, peeled and
   finely chopped
2 garlic cloves, finely chopped
5 spring onions [scallions], finely chopped
3 Tbsp toasted sesame seeds
2 Tbsp toasted sesame oil, for frying

For the noodle soup
2 Tbsp olive oil
3 garlic cloves, finely chopped
½ thumb of ginger, peeled and chopped
1 Tbsp Thai red curry paste
1 litre [4½ cups] chicken or fish
   stock [broth]
2 tsp fish sauce
440ml [1¾ cups] coconut milk
200g [7oz] dried rice vermicelli noodles

To serve
1 lime, cut into wedges
1 red chilli, sliced
1 small bunch of coriander [cilantro],
   roughly chopped

To make the dumplings, add the fish to a food processor along with the soy, fish sauce and lime juice, and pulse until broken up into a thick paste. Tip into a large bowl and mix together with the chilli, ginger, garlic, 3 of the spring onions, and the sesame seeds. Roll into walnut-sized balls and set aside.

Heat the sesame oil in a frying pan and fry the fish balls in batches until cooked through, about 8–10 minutes, moving constantly so they are golden all over.

To make the noodle soup, heat the olive oil in a saucepan, add the garlic, ginger and curry paste and fry for a minute or so. Add the stock, fish sauce and coconut milk, bring to a simmer, then add the noodles. Turn off the heat and leave until the noodles are just cooked, stirring occasionally so they don't stick together.

To serve, divide the soup among 4 bowls and add the dumplings. Serve with a squeeze of lime and scatter with the chilli, the remaining spring onions, and the chopped coriander.

[SERVES 4]

This is really a very simple recipe with plenty of room for experimentation. Try upping the lentil quantity and using less meat or perhaps adding some dried chilli to the mix or sauce for an extra kick. Take care not to overcook the lentils as the mushier they get, the more difficult it will be for the meatballs to hold their shape. I love that these are oven-baked – it means no constant hovering over the frying pan and makes for a much healthier meal.

3. Lamb meatballs

with lentils & cumin

[YOU WILL NEED]

olive oil, for greasing
100g [generous ½ cup] red lentils
300g [1⅓ cups] lean lamb mince [ground lamb]
1 onion, grated
2 garlic cloves, finely chopped
1 egg, beaten
1 tsp ground cumin
½ tsp fennel seeds
1 tsp dried oregano
1 tsp dried thyme
400g [generous 2 cups] couscous, cooked to packet instructions, to serve

For the tomato sauce
1 Tbsp olive oil
1 red onion, finely chopped
1 garlic clove, finely chopped
½ tsp ground cumin
½ tsp smoked paprika
1 tsp ground cinnamon
1 Tbsp tomato purée [paste]
1 Tbsp red wine vinegar
400g [2 cups] canned chopped tomatoes
1 small bunch of parsley, roughly chopped
1 small bunch of coriander [cilantro], roughly chopped, plus extra leaves to garnish

Preheat the oven to 200°C/400°F and generously grease a baking sheet with a little oil. Cook the lentils according to the packet instructions. Drain well and leave to cool a little. Tip into a large bowl with the lamb, onion, garlic, egg, spices and herbs. Season generously and combine to form a very wet mixture.

Roll the mixture into balls (grease your hands with a little oil to make a little easier), about 3cm [1¼in] in diameter, and place onto the prepared baking sheet. Bake for 20 minutes until golden and cooked through.

Meanwhile, make the tomato sauce. Heat the olive oil in a medium frying pan and fry the onion over a low-medium heat until soft, about 10 minutes. Add the garlic and spices and fry until toasted and fragrant. Add the tomato purée and cook for a minute or two, then add the vinegar and cook for a further minute. Tip in the chopped tomatoes and a ladleful of water and simmer for 20 minutes until thickened. Carefully stir through the meatballs and the herbs. Serve on top of the couscous garnished with extra coriander.

[SERVES 4]

This is a real favourite. It's a sort of cross between a lasagne and a quiche, with a crumbly, wholemeal pastry and a rich, meaty filling. Because it is made with mince, the filling itself doesn't take too long to cook. Serve with a salad for supper and pack any leftovers for tomorrow's lunch.

Köttfärspaj

[*Hearty beef quiche*]

[YOU WILL NEED]

175g [scant 1⅓ cups] wholemeal [whole-wheat] flour
125g [9 Tbsp] butter, cold and cubed
1 Tbsp cold-pressed rapeseed oil or olive oil
1 onion, finely chopped
200g [3⅓ cups] mushrooms, sliced
2 garlic cloves, finely chopped
400g [1¾ cups] beef mince [ground beef]
1 tsp dried oregano
1 tsp dried thyme
¼ tsp paprika
2 Tbsp tomato purée [paste]
1 Tbsp plain [all-purpose] flour
2 eggs, beaten
50g [½ cup] grated Cheddar cheese

[SERVES 6-8]

Pulse the flour, butter and a pinch of sea salt in a food processor until it resembles breadcrumbs. Gradually add 3-4 tablespoons of ice-cold water, pulsing between additions and scraping the sides of the mixer bowl to make sure you get any stuck wet bits of dough. Bring the dough together with your hands on a lightly floured work surface, then wrap in clingfilm. Chill in the fridge while you make the filling.

Preheat the oven to 220°C/425°F. Heat the oil in a large frying pan and gently cook the onion until soft and translucent, about 10 minutes. Add the mushrooms and fry until golden, stirring frequently for about 4 minutes. Tip in the garlic and cook for another few minutes. Transfer the mixture to a plate, then fry the beef for 5–7 minutes until browned. Season and then return the vegetables to the pan. Stir through the herbs, paprika, tomato purée and flour. Cook for about 3 minutes, then pour in 125ml [½ cup] water and remove from the heat.

Roll out the dough on a lightly floured surface and use to line a 24-cm [9½-in] fluted pie dish. Blind bake by scrunching up a circle of greaseproof baking parchment and placing on top of the dough. Fill with baking beans, dried beans or rice. Bake for about 10 minutes until golden, then remove the baking parchment and beans.

Stir the eggs and grated cheese through the beef mixture, then spoon into the pie case. Reduce the oven temperature to 180°C/350°F and bake for 20–25 minutes, until golden and the filling is cooked through. Serve with a crunchy salad, dressed with a sharp mustardy dressing.

This recipe may, on the face of it, not seem particularly noteworthy, but it is one of my favourites. Cod and prawns are a common duo in Swedish dishes (often served with horseradish and chopped boiled eggs to garnish) so this is a bit of a twist on a traditional offering. Sage and fish might not be an obvious pairing, but here it really works, especially with a helping hand lent by the lemon and garlic to add a sharp freshness. If you'd like to go lighter, use sweet potatoes and a few scant tablespoons of olive oil instead of the brown butter.

Baked cod & prawns

with browned sage butter & garlic mash

[YOU WILL NEED]

1kg [2¼lb] floury [mealy] potatoes, peeled and halved if very large
4 garlic cloves, peeled
4 x 175g [6oz] thick cod fillets
1 lemon, zest and juice
1 small bunch of dill, roughly chopped
3 Tbsp olive oil
200ml [scant 1 cup] milk
freshly ground white pepper
60g [4½ Tbsp] butter
1 small bunch of sage, leaves picked and finely chopped
200g [7oz] cooked Atlantic prawns [shrimp], fresh or frozen and thawed

[SERVES 4]

Preheat the oven to 180°C/350°F. Place the potatoes and garlic in a large pan and cover with cold water. Bring to the boil, then reduce the heat and simmer for 30 minutes until soft and cooked through.

Just before the potatoes are done, place each cod fillet on a square of foil and season with salt and pepper. Squeeze over a little lemon juice and sprinkle over the zest and a little dill. Wrap up the foil packages and transfer to a baking sheet. Bake for 20 minutes, until the fish is just cooked through and flaky.

Drain the potatoes and garlic and return to the pan to steam-dry. Mash roughly, taking care to evenly distribute the garlic, then stir in the olive oil and milk. Season with salt and white pepper.

Melt the butter in a large pan and cook over a low heat until the milk solids begin to brown and smell nutty. Add the sage leaves and cook for a few seconds until crisping up, then tip in the prawns. Cook for a minute or two until heated through. Add a squeeze of lemon juice and some salt, pepper and the remaining dill. Serve the cod with the mash and top with the prawns and sage butter.

This is a lovely way to lift a simple roast chicken to a feast-worthy meal. The quince glaze adds a sweetness while also crisping up the chicken skin. I like to serve this in late autumn when quinces are just coming into season and the days are getting shorter. This promises to cheer.

Quince-glazed chicken

———

with fig & walnut stuffing, & smashed butter beans

[YOU WILL NEED]

500g [1lb 2oz] quinces, cored and cut
    into wedges
200g [1 cup] caster [granulated] sugar
1½ lemons, zest and juice
3 Tbsp extra virgin olive oil, plus a little
    extra for drizzling
1 onion, finely chopped
100g [⅔ cup] dried figs, finely chopped
50g [generous ⅓ cup] walnuts, finely
    chopped
50g [3½ Tbsp] butter, softened
60g [1 cup] fresh breadcrumbs
3 thyme sprigs, leaves picked and
    chopped
1 small bunch of parsley, finely chopped
1 small bunch of sage, finely chopped
pinch of ground nutmeg
1 tsp ground ginger
1 tsp ground cinnamon
1.8–2kg [4–4½lb] chicken, best quality
    you can afford
2 x 400g [2⅓ cups] cans butter
    [lima] beans
rocket [arugula], to serve

[SERVES 4–6]

Place the quince in a large pan with the sugar, 1½ tablespoons lemon juice and 500ml [generous 2 cups] water. Bring to the boil, then lower the heat and simmer until reduced to a light syrup, about 1 hour. Remove the quince, setting aside about half the wedges (save for a compote or pudding another time), but reserving the rest.

Preheat the oven to 190°C/375°F. Heat 1 tablespoon olive oil in a small pan and add the onion. Sweat over a low heat until translucent, then tip into a bowl with the figs, walnuts and butter. Remove the skin from the reserved quinces and mash the flesh. Add this to the bowl and mix in the breadcrumbs, most of the chopped herbs and all the spices.

Fill the chicken cavity with the stuffing, leaving a little room at the opening. Drizzle with olive oil and sprinkle with sea salt. Place the chicken in a roasting tray and roast for 20 minutes per 500g [1lb 2oz].

After the cooking time, remove from the oven and baste with the quince glaze, then return to the oven for a further 15 minutes. Baste again before serving.

Tip the beans into a saucepan with a splash of water, the remaining 2 tablespoons of oil, lemon juice and zest and the remaining herbs. Mash together until creamy over a low heat then season with salt and pepper.

Carve the chicken and serve with the smashed beans and some rocket.

Call this a Scandi Caesar salad, if you like. It has that familiar crisp crunch of lettuce and croûtons and the same bite from the acidity of the dressing. This version is definitely a lot lighter, with crème fraîche to account for most of that distinctive creaminess in the dressing. Tarragon and mackerel are great friends but if you would prefer to use some roast chicken, this would work too and would be a great way to use up leftovers.

Grilled mackerel salad

—

with sourdough croûtons, tarragon Caesar dressing & quick pickled red onion

[YOU WILL NEED]

1 red onion, thinly sliced
2 Tbsp white wine vinegar
pinch of sugar
2 thick slices of sourdough bread, torn
   into bite-sized chunks
2 Tbsp olive oil
2 garlic cloves, finely chopped
½ lemon, zest and juice
1 Tbsp cold-pressed rapeseed oil or olive
   oil, plus a little extra for brushing
2 Tbsp light crème fraîche
1 Tbsp mayonnaise
5 tarragon leaves, finely chopped
4 mackerel fillets, pin-boned
2 large heads romaine or cos lettuce,
   torn into pieces
25g [1oz] Parmesan cheese, shaved

[SERVES 4]

Start by making the pickled onion. Place the sliced red onion in a small bowl and sprinkle with 1 tablespoon of the vinegar. Sprinkle over a little sea salt and a pinch sugar. Stir, then set aside for at least 20 minutes, until the onions have turned bright pink and have lost their bite.

Preheat the oven to 200°C/400°F. Place the bread chunks on a baking sheet, drizzle with 1 tablespoon of the olive oil and season with salt and pepper. Toss to coat really well then space the bread out evenly on the sheet. Bake for 10–12 minutes, turning halfway through until crisped-up and golden.

Make the dressing by mixing the garlic and remaining vinegar together. Leave for 5 minutes, then add the lemon juice, zest and rapeseed oil. Stir through the crème fraîche, mayonnaise and tarragon.

Heat the grill [broiler] and line a baking sheet with foil. Place the mackerel fillets on the prepared baking sheet, skin side up. Brush with a little rapeseed oil and season with salt and pepper. Grill for 5 minutes, then flip over and grill for another few minutes until cooked through.

Toss the lettuce, dressing, Parmesan shavings and croûtons together in a large salad bowl. Divide among 4 plates, scatter with the pickled onions and top with the mackerel.

Pheasants can seem a bit intimidating to cook if you are not familiar with game birds – they don't exactly look appealing and the threat of overcooking and ending up with dry meat looms large. This recipe could really not be simpler. Spatchcocking the pheasants is a breezy process and makes cooking quick and even. The smothering here refers to the buttery massage they receive before cooking which also stops them drying out. This is a wonderfully wintery recipe to impress (with very little effort on your part). The cabbage is based on my mother's recipe – a Christmas favourite.

Smothered pheasant

———

with apples, prunes & the best braised red cabbage

[YOU WILL NEED]

100g [¾ cup] prunes, stoned
2 pheasants
50g [3½ Tbsp] butter
1 small bunch of thyme, leaves picked,
    plus a few sprigs
1 lemon, zest
3 small cooking apples, quartered
2 onions, cut into wedges

For the red cabbage
1 tsp butter
1 onion, sliced
1 head of red cabbage, finely sliced
4–5 tart apples, cored and sliced into
    half moons
6 cloves
4 black peppercorns, crushed
2 Tbsp red wine vinegar
2 Tbsp honey
2 Tbsp redcurrant jelly
150ml [⅔ cup] red wine

[SERVES 4]

Cover the prunes with water in a small bowl and set aside while you prepare the cabbage.

Melt the butter in your largest saucepan and fry the onion for 5 minutes without colouring. Add the cabbage, apples, spices, vinegar, honey and 1 teaspoon sea salt. Stir well, clamp on a lid and cook over a low heat for 45 minutes, stirring and checking every so often. Add the redcurrant jelly and red wine and cook for a further 45 minutes, or until the cabbage is soft and almost jammy.

Preheat the oven to 200°C/400°F. Spatchcock the pheasants by cutting out the backbone with a pair of sharp kitchen scissors. Flatten the bird out with your hands so you hear a "crack". Mix the butter with the thyme, lemon zest and plenty of seasoning.

Place the pheasants in a large roasting tray and scatter the apples, onion, a few thyme sprigs and the drained prunes around the birds. Massage the pheasants with the butter so they are well coated and then season. Roast for 30–40 minutes, basting at least twice, until golden.

Serve with the roasted apples, onions and prunes, as well as the red cabbage.

FREDAGSMYS

Three recipes for cosy Fridays

---

[1] Wild tacos with venison, pickled red onion, grilled guacamole, coriander & feta
[2] Salmon burgers with crunchy corn salsa, & lime & jalapeño mayo
[3] Spelt pizza with mushrooms, potatoes & fresh cheese

Swedish winters are long, dark and cold. It can be really difficult to leave the sofa when it's utterly freezing outside. When my friend, Axel, first moved to London for work, I asked him how he was finding it compared to Stockholm. "It's great," he replied. "In the winter, you can make plans after work to go out, go to the pub or for a meal. In Stockholm it's too cold."

This was perhaps a slight exaggeration but the Swedes have developed some excellent coping strategies for the winter months. They dress properly, prepare their homes and vehicles and adjust their routines. And then there's *fredagsmys*. Roughly translated as "cosy Friday" this phenomenon has been going since the 90s, driven by an advertising campaign by one of the main snack brands (complete with a catchy song). The idea was that you hunkered down with your family and indulged in front of a film or TV programme. Favourite foods include pizza, noodles, popcorn and pick 'n' mix sweets. But the most popular dish, by far, is tacos.

Having tacos, complete with all the sauces and sides, on a Friday is a Swedish institution. There are supermarket aisles dedicated to *fredagsmys* with Tex Mex at the centre. And who can blame the Swedes – it's delicious.

I love the idea of elevating Friday evening to something special, a chance to spend time together and relax after a busy week with some indulgent, comforting food. Here are some of my versions of *fredagsmys* favourites, with a slightly lighter twist.

"Since I moved here, all I do is *mys* and *mys*"

[FROM THE *FREDAGSMYS* SONG BY
CRISP MANUFACTURER OWL, CIRCA 2009]

In Swedish, all game comes under the term vilt *(wild) and includes elk, moose, reindeer and boar. These are generally served in quite hearty dishes – think plenty of potato and gravy. However, they work equally well with spices. Venison meat, in particular, pairs really well with the warmth of the taco spices in this recipe, though you can of course substitute with beef steak. Grilling the avocados gives the guacamole a lovely smoky flavour and elevates it to something a bit special.*

1. Wild tacos

———

with venison, pickled red onion, grilled guacamole, coriander & feta

[YOU WILL NEED]

1½ Tbsp dried oregano
2 tsp ground cumin
2 tsp ground coriander
2 tsp paprika
pinch of chilli [red pepper] flakes
½ tsp sugar
2 garlic cloves, finely chopped
1 lime, zest and juice
3 Tbsp cold-pressed rapeseed oil or olive oil,
    plus extra for frying
600g [1¼lb] venison steaks

For the guacamole
2 ripe avocados
1 lime, zest and juice
½ red onion, finely chopped
1 small handful of coriander [cilantro],
    stalks and leaves finely chopped
pinch of chilli [red pepper] flakes

To serve
Pickled Red Onion (see page 98)
small soft corn tortillas or taco shells
sliced pickled or fresh chillies
rocket [arugula]
lime wedges
coriander [cilantro], roughly chopped
feta, crumbled

[SERVES 4]

Begin by making the marinade. In a large bowl, combine all of the spices with the sugar and plenty of salt and pepper. Tip in the garlic, lime juice and zest and whisk together with the oil. Trim any fat and sinew off the venison steaks, then turn the steaks in the marinade to coat well. Cover with clingfilm and refrigerate for at least 3 hours, but ideally overnight.

Heat a little oil in a large frying pan and fry the steaks for 4–5 minutes on each side for medium-rare, more for very thick steaks. Set aside covered with a little foil or baking parchment to rest while you make the guacamole.

Heat a griddle pan to scorching hot. Halve, peel and stone the avocados and place cut side down on the griddle. Grill until charred and starting to soften, about 4 minutes, then flip over and repeat on the other side. Remove and allow to cool.

Roughly mash the avocados in a bowl with a generous pinch of sea salt, pepper and the lime juice. Add the lime zest, red onion, coriander and chilli flakes and taste to adjust the seasoning.

Slice the steaks thinly and place on a platter, sprinkled with a few coriander leaves. Serve with the guacamole, pickled onion and all of the accoutrements, allowing your guests to get stuck in.

Like the tacos recipe, this is an interactive dish. Half the fun is building your own burger, seeing how high you can pile the salsa, sauce and extras – salad, veg, onions, pickles, whatever you fancy. And while this burger will feel decadent, it isn't particularly unhealthy, especially if you omit the buns in favour of some big crunchy leaves of cos or romaine lettuce. But even with the buns, there's still a lot of good stuff here (vegetables, salmon, decent fats and lots of punchy flavour). Just go easy on the mayo if you want a lighter meal.

2. Salmon burgers

with crunchy corn salsa, & lime & jalapeño mayo

[YOU WILL NEED]

For the burgers
4 skinless salmon fillets, approx.
  120g [4¼oz] each
1 small bunch of coriander [cilantro]
1 egg, beaten
50g [scant 1 cup] fresh wholemeal
  [whole-wheat] breadcrumbs
1 red chilli, finely chopped
1 lime, zest and juice
cold-pressed rapeseed oil or olive oil,
  for frying
4 burger buns or large lettuce leaves, to serve

For the salsa
2 fresh corn-on-the-cobs
1 small red onion, finely chopped
1 green chilli, finely chopped
1 green [bell] pepper, roughly chopped
2 Tbsp olive oil
1 Tbsp red wine vinegar
½ tsp smoked paprika

For the mayonnaise
2 egg yolks
1 fat garlic clove, crushed
1 pickled jalapeño pepper, finely chopped
1 lime, zest and juice
300ml [1¼ cups] cold-pressed rapeseed oil
  or vegetable oil

For the burgers, finely chop the salmon and the stems from the coriander (reserve the leaves for the salsa). Place in a large bowl with the egg, breadcrumbs, chilli, and lime zest and juice. Season and mix to combine. Alternatively, blitz briefly in a food processor until the mixture comes together. Form into 4 rounded patties and set aside.

For the salsa, cut the corn kernels from the cobs and place in a bowl. Roughly chop the reserved coriander leaves and add to the bowl of corn with the red onion, chilli and green pepper. Make a quick dressing by whisking together the olive oil, vinegar, paprika and a little salt and pepper. Dress the salsa and set aside while you make the mayonnaise.

Place the egg yolks into a large bowl with the garlic, jalapeño pepper and lime juice and zest and whisk with electric beaters while you slowly pour in the oil, trickling it into the mixture in a thin stream until you have a thick mayonnaise. Pop in the fridge.

Heat a generous glug of oil in a large frying pan and fry the salmon burgers over a medium heat for 7 minutes on each side until golden and cooked through.

Serve in the buns or lettuce leaves with the mayonnaise and salsa along with any combination of extras, such as lettuce, tomato, red onion, cucumber, pickled gherkins, sliced avocado, capers and tomato chutney.

[SERVES 4]

This quick pizza dough doesn't require any rising, so it's a breeze to prepare. You can speed up the process even further by using a fresh cheese like ricotta if you don't want to make your own. This is really just a take on a pizza bianca but it would work just as well with a tomato base and some cured meat for a more Mediterranean-style topping.

3. Spelt pizza

with mushrooms, potatoes & fresh cheese

[YOU WILL NEED]

For the fresh cheese
2 litres [8 cups] whole milk
2–3 Tbsp lemon juice or white
   wine vinegar
1 lemon, zest and juice

For the pizza
350g [2⅔ cups] wholemeal [whole-wheat]
   spelt flour
1 Tbsp baking powder
2 tsp dried oregano
1½ Tbsp cold-pressed rapeseed oil or
   olive oil, plus a little extra for drizzling
3–4 [250g/8¾oz] small potatoes, very
   thinly sliced (ideally with a mandoline)
150g [2½ cups] mixed mushrooms, sliced
2 rosemary sprigs, leaves picked
1 large handful of rocket [arugula],
   to serve
Parmesan, shaved, to serve

[SERVES 4]

To make the cheese, place the milk in a large saucepan with 1 teaspoon sea salt. Slowly bring to the boil then immediately remove from the heat. Add the 2–3 tablespoons of lemon juice or vinegar and stir until you can see the mixture splitting into curds and whey. If this doesn't happen, add more vinegar or lemon.

Strain the mixture through a sieve lined with muslin [cheesecloth]. If you have a bag for making jelly or nut milks, you can also use this. Squeeze the muslin or bag a little and discard the resulting liquid, but it shouldn't be too dry. Tip into a bowl with the lemon zest, a squeeze of the juice and a little seasoning. Place a plate directly on the curds and weigh down with a couple of heavy cans. Chill for at least 2 hours. The cheese is now ready to eat and will keep in the fridge for up to a week (stir in a little milk if it is not creamy enough).

Preheat the oven to 220°C/425°F and lightly grease 2 baking sheets. For the pizza, mix the flour, baking powder, oregano and 1 teaspoon sea salt in a large bowl. Place 250ml [1 cup] "finger warm" (just warm to touch) water in a jug with the oil and slowly add this to the dry ingredients, mixing constantly. The mixture should come together to form a dough, but if very dry, mix in a little more water.

Divide the pizza dough in half and flatten to form ovals on the prepared baking sheets. Spread the cheese over the bases and top with the thinly sliced potato. Scatter over the mushrooms and rosemary and drizzle over some oil and seasoning. Bake for 17–20 minutes, until puffed up and golden, swapping the trays halfway through cooking so that they both get some of the heat from the top of the oven. Serve topped with rocket and shaved Parmesan.

Crayfish are revered in Sweden. It used to be permitted to fish them only for a short period in August, so they were celebrated around this time by throwing crayfish parties. A bit like a crawfish boil in the States, the crustaceans themselves are an excuse to celebrate. We like to simply boil ours with plenty of dill and serve with crispbread, strong västerbotten *cheese quiche, and an endless supply of beer and snaps. There should also be colourful paper hats, bibs and drinking songs. Them's the rules.*

Avocado & crayfish spelt spaghetti

——

with lemon, dill & rye crumbs

[YOU WILL NEED]

300g [10½oz] wholemeal [whole-wheat]
   spelt spaghetti
olive oil, for frying and tossing
1 garlic clove, finely chopped
2 slices of rye bread, blitzed into crumbs
1 lemon, zest and juice
3 avocados, peeled, halved and stoned
300g [10½oz] cooked crayfish tails
1 handful of basil, roughly chopped
1 small bag of rocket [arugula]
Parmesan, shaved, to serve

[SERVES 4]

Cook the pasta according to the packet instructions, reserving a little of the hot, starchy cooking water. Meanwhile, heat a good glug of olive oil in a large frying pan and fry the garlic for about 30 seconds. Stir in the rye crumbs and lemon zest and fry until starting to brown and crisp up. Set aside.

Blitz all but one half of one of the avocados in a food processor, along with a splash of the pasta water, plenty of sea salt and a squeeze of lemon juice. Cube the remaining avocado half and squeeze over a little bit of lemon juice.

Toss the pasta with a little olive oil, then add the crayfish, basil and avocado sauce. Top with the rocket, avocado cubes, shaved Parmesan and rye crumbs.

*NOTE crayfish

Crayfish are of course available all year round these days and in most countries the tails can be easily found lightly brined. This recipe is an idea for when you can't get hold of the real deal and want a quick seafood fix. You could of course also use prawns.

Although I have already offered a fried herring recipe in this book, I feel there is room for another one – this time more traditional. The chips in question aren't chips so much as mash, which is as much of a staple to our fried herring as chips are to British fried cod. Here, the shallots play the role of a crisp, crunchy element instead. These could also be served with lingonberry jam, as they often are in Sweden, lending sweetness to counteract the dish's saltiness. Don't knock it till you've tried it.

Scandi fish & chips

—

[Fried herring with Nobis sauce & crispy shallots]

[YOU WILL NEED]

1kg [2¼lb] floury [mealy] potatoes, peeled and cut into chunks
100ml [7 Tbsp] milk
1 tsp butter
3 Tbsp crème fraîche
white pepper
8 herring fillets, pin-boned (ask your fishmonger)
4 tsp Dijon mustard
1 small bunch of curly parsley, finely chopped
50g [⅔ cup] dried breadcrumbs
50g [½ cup] rye flour
olive or vegetable oil, for frying
2 shallots, finely sliced
3 Tbsp cornflour [cornstarch]
thinly sliced cucumber

For the Nobis sauce
1 medium egg
2 tsp white wine vinegar
1 tsp Dijon mustard
100ml [7 tbsp] olive oil
1 small bunch of chives, finely chopped

[SERVES 4]

Place the potatoes in a large pan and cover with water. Bring to a simmer and cook until soft, about 15–20 minutes. Once cooked, drain and return to the pan to steam-dry. Mash well, then mix in the milk, butter and crème fraîche. Season with salt and white pepper.

Next, prepare the Nobis sauce. Boil the egg for 3 minutes, then drain and rinse under cold running water to cool down – the egg must be soft-boiled. Peel and place in a blender with the vinegar and Dijon mustard. With the motor running, slowly pour in the olive oil until you end up with a thick sauce. Stir through the chives and season with salt and pepper.

Lay half the herring fillets on a board, skin side down. Brush with the mustard, sprinkle over the parsley and season with salt and pepper. Sandwich together with the other fillets.

Mix the breadcrumbs and flour together with plenty of seasoning. Dredge the herring in the mixture on both sides then heat the oil in a large frying pan. Fry for about 4–5 minutes on each side until golden and cooked through.

Toss the shallots in cornflour, then heat a good glug of oil in a small frying pan. Fry over a medium heat until crispy then leave to drain on kitchen paper.

Serve the herring topped with the crispy shallots and a side of mash, Nobis sauce, plus a little thinly sliced cucumber.

SÖTT
[desserts]

It is no secret that the Swedes have a sweet tooth. The very fact that we have the word *fika* (to describe the act of sitting down with a cup of coffee and something sweet) goes to prove that we do not deprive ourselves of life's temptations. However, we approach these things with a healthy dose of moderation. When I was growing up, desserts were not something you had every day. They didn't complete a meal either. They were something extra and special, perhaps on a weekend, for a celebration or when you had friends over for supper.

If you ever have the pleasure of being invited to a Swedish dinner party, don't necessarily expect a relaxed affair. We take pride in showing off our kitchen skills, homes and tables. There's a formality to these events that often takes the uninitiated by surprise. Even raising a glass follows a strict protocol – eye contact is key. Desserts are the final flourish, of course. I remember my mother spending months planning her Midsummer's Eve dinner menu and dessert was always the most carefully considered. One memorable year, she even made a cake involving thin layers of potatoes, which felt particularly elaborate.

Not all desserts have to be quite so complicated, of course. One of my favourites as a child was *marängsviss* ("meringue Swiss"). It was a simple and extremely decadent sundae with layers of crumbled meringue, ice cream, chocolate sauce and whipped cream. I have no idea what this had to do with Switzerland, but the fact that it had such a grand name only raised its reverence in my mind.

The recipes in this chapter have been created with this in mind – most are not particularly complicated to make, but are to be honoured and relished. In the spirit of *lagom*, if the rest of your meals have been healthy and you decide to have dessert, you should enjoy it wholeheartedly without even the slightest hint of guilt.

This is inspired by one of my favourite childhood stories about Pettson and his cat, Findus. It's the cat's birthday and Pettson wants to make him a pancake cake. For this he needs flour which means going to the shop. So he needs his bicycle, which has a flat tyre and the pump is locked in a shed. The shed key is at the bottom of a well so he needs a ladder, which is in a field with an angry bull. So he has to distract the bull to get the ladder, to get the key, to get the pump, to... you get the picture. Happily, the cat does finally get the cake. I have to say, it is well worth the effort.

Celebration pancake cake

——

layered with cream & blueberry compote

[YOU WILL NEED]

400g [3 cups] plain [all-purpose] flour
4 eggs, beaten
250ml [1 cup] milk
4 tbsp melted butter, plus more for frying
2 lemons, zest and juice
300ml [1¼ cups] double [heavy] cream
caster [superfine] sugar, to taste (optional)
blueberry jam, or your favourite jam
    (raspberry and strawberry also
    work well)
200g [1½ cups] blueberries, to serve
mint, to decorate (optional)

[SERVES 8]

To make the pancake batter, sift the flour into a large bowl along with a pinch of salt. Make a well and add the eggs, milk, butter and 250ml [1 cup] water. Whisk together until you have a thick batter. Add most of the lemon zest and a squeeze of the juice. Set aside for about 10 minutes to let any bubbles or lumps of flour settle.

Melt a little butter in a hot frying pan about 16cm [6in] in diameter and add half a ladleful of the batter. Immediately swirl the pan around to evenly disperse the mixture. Once bubbles start to appear on the surface and the bottom seems dry, flip the pancake over using a spatula. Fry for another minute or so. The first pancake is likely to be a disaster – this is the universal pancake rule. Eat it immediately sprinkled with sugar and then carry on making more pancakes until you have used up all the batter.

Allow your pancakes to cool completely on a wire rack. This is important, as warm pancakes will mean a melty, messy filling. Whip the cream quite stiffly, adding a little squeeze of lemon juice and any remaining zest. Sweeten with sugar if you like. Layer the pancakes on a serving plate, alternating with the jam, cream and blueberries. Finish by spreading the top layer with cream, drizzling over some more jam and decorating with more blueberries, lemon zest and a sprig of mint, if you like. To serve, slice like a cake.

Blueberry ice cream

with buttermilk

[YOU WILL NEED]

200g [scant 1⅔ cups] fresh blueberries
150g [generous ¾ cup] caster
    [superfine] sugar
500ml [generous 2 cups] double
    [heavy] cream
1 vanilla pod [bean], split in half
    lengthways
300ml [1¼ cups] buttermilk

[MAKES 500ML (1 PINT)]

Place the blueberries in a small saucepan with half the sugar and simmer over a low heat, until the sugar has dissolved and the blueberries have disintegrated, about 10 minutes. Allow to cool.

Tip the remaining sugar, cream and vanilla into another pan and bring to a simmer, stirring until you can no longer feel any grainy granules of sugar. Cool completely.

Tip the buttermilk into a large bowl and add the cream and blueberry mixtures. Stir together until well combined, then churn in an ice-cream maker according to the manufacturer's instructions. Freeze in a suitable container. Alternatively, if you don't have an ice-cream maker, freeze for 3 hours, stirring to break up the ice crystals every 40 minutes.

Cardamom rice pudding

with sour cherry compote

[YOU WILL NEED]

750ml [3 cups] semi-skimmed [low-fat] milk
5 cardamom pods, split open and
    seeds bashed
2 cinnamon sticks
50g [¼ cup] caster [superfine] sugar
100g [½ cup] pudding [short-grain] rice
3 Tbsp crème fraîche
2 Tbsp toasted flaked [slivered] almonds,
    to serve

For the sour cherry compote
200g [7oz] frozen sour cherries (or black
    cherries if unavailable), stoned
75g [6 Tbsp] caster [superfine] sugar
1 star anise
1 orange, zest and juice

[SERVES 4]

Pour the milk into a large saucepan and add the cardamom, 1 of the cinnamon sticks and the sugar. Bring to a simmer, then reduce the heat and cook gently, stirring until the sugar has dissolved. Remove from the heat and leave to infuse for about 1 hour.

To make the sour cherry compote, place all the ingredients, along with the remaining cinnamon stick, in a medium saucepan. Bring to a gentle simmer and cook for 15–20 minutes until reduced and syrupy. Remove the star anise and cinnamon stick.

Add the rice to the infused milk and bring to the boil. Reduce the heat and simmer for 20 minutes, stirring frequently, until the rice is cooked and everything is creamy. Remove the cinnamon stick and stir through the crème fraîche. Serve with the compote and sprinkled with the toasted almonds.

SUMMER STRAWBERRIES

Three recipes to celebrate summer

---

[1] A strawberry cake for Midsummer's Eve
[2] Strawberry ice cream with crème fraîche & rosewater
[3] Strawberry compote with black pepper

Strawberries are an essential part of the Swedish summer, making their premiere around the time of Midsummer's Eve in late June. This originally pagan holiday to honour the summer solstice is second only to Christmas in terms of festive importance. At both times of year, food and feasting are central. Midsummer would not be quite the same without a strawberry cake and cup of coffee after lunch to soak up all the herring, snaps and beer.

Swedish strawberries are smaller than many imported varieties, very juicy and super-sweet – I cannot sing their praises enough. They are sold everywhere – we frequently stop off on the way out to the countryside to pick up a punnet or two from a roadside stall. Most prized are *smultron* – wild strawberries – which look like cute, mini strawberries but have a much more concentrated, intense and heady flavour.

Swedish strawberries have a relatively short season, but we make the most of it by gorging on them throughout the summer, most often served simply, perhaps with a dollop of cream or scoop of ice cream. However, we also work them into lots of our desserts and preserves to celebrate their brief but impactful appearance.

"Sommaren är kort det mesta regnar bort"
["Summer is short, most of it rains away"]

SONG BY TOMAS LEDIN

This is a classic Swedish cake that is made up and down the country through the summer months, in particular for Midsummer's Eve. It also happens to be the cake that I have every year for my birthday in July. It consists of a sponge made without added fat, which I think makes it a lot more straightforward – there is no risk of splitting the creamed sugar and butter when the eggs are added. Instead the eggs and sugar are whisked until custard-coloured and airy before adding the dry ingredients. The result is an extra-light, fluffy sponge which soaks up any strawberry juices really well or, in this case, a minty syrup.

1. A strawberry cake

for Midsummer's Eve

[YOU WILL NEED]

For the cake
butter, for greasing
4 large eggs
175g [1 cup] caster [superfine] sugar
1 tsp vanilla extract or ½ tsp vanilla
    powder or paste
100g [¾ cup] plain [all-purpose] flour
40g [scant ½ cup] cornflour [cornstarch]
    or potato flour
1 tsp baking powder

For the syrup
75g [scant ½ cup] caster [superfine] sugar
1 lemon, zest and juice
1 bunch of mint, roughly chopped

For the filling & decoration
400g [4 cups] strawberries
2 Tbsp caster [superfine] sugar
250ml [1 cup] double [heavy] or
    whipping cream
dash of vanilla extract, powder or paste
1 small bunch of mint, leaves picked
    (optional)

[SERVES 8]

Preheat the oven to 175°C/350°F and move a shelf to the bottom. Grease and line a 24-cm [9½-in] round, loose-bottom cake tin. To make the cake, in a large bowl, whisk the eggs and sugar until pale and creamy. Add the vanilla.

Mix the flours and baking powder in a small bowl, then fold into the egg mixture, carefully incorporating all the ingredients. Pour into the prepared tin and bake on the bottom shelf for 30 minutes, until risen, golden and a cake tester comes out clean. Cool a little before releasing from the tin, then move to a wire rack to cool completely.

Make the syrup by combining the sugar, lemon juice, zest, mint and 200ml [scant 1 cup] water in a small saucepan. Heat gently until the sugar has dissolved, then bring to a simmer for about 5 minutes. Cool completely before straining into a jug.

For the filling and decoration, hull half the strawberries and chop. Place in a bowl with the sugar and mash together with a fork to form a rough fresh jam. Halve the remaining strawberries, keeping their stalks on. Whip the cream quite loosely – take care not to overwhip! Stir through the vanilla.

Split the cooled cake in half through the middle. I like to trace the outline with a knife, all the way around the side, then use a long piece of strong thread to cut through the cake.

To assemble, drizzle the bottom layer of cake with half the syrup. Spread with the strawberry jam and half the whipped cream. Top with the remaining cake layer and drizzle this with more syrup. Decorate with the last of the cream, the halved strawberries and mint sprigs, if desired.

2. Strawberry ice cream

———

with crème fraîche & rosewater

[YOU WILL NEED]

500g [5 cups] strawberries, hulled
200g [generous 1 cup] caster
   [superfine] sugar
few drops of rosewater
500ml [generous 2 cups] full-fat
   crème fraîche
chopped pistachios (optional), to serve

[MAKES 500ML (1 PINT)]

Blitz the strawberries and sugar in a food processor to make a coulis, then strain through a fine-mesh sieve. Add a couple of drops of rosewater, tasting to make sure the rose does not overpower the strawberry flavour.

Combine two-thirds of the coulis with the crème fraîche, mixing well, then churn in an ice-cream maker, following the manufacturer's instructions. Swirl the remaining coulis through the ice cream right before freezing. If you don't have an ice-cream maker, tip into a freezerproof tub and freeze for 1 hour. Mix thoroughly to break up the ice crystals, then return to the freezer for another hour. Repeat this process a further 2–3 times. Swirl the coulis through the ice cream before the final freezing stage.

Serve sprinkled with pistachios, if desired, or scooped into cones.

---

3. Strawberry compote

———

with black pepper

[YOU WILL NEED]

500g [5 cups] strawberries, hulled and
   quartered
50g [¼ cup] caster [superfine] sugar
½ lemon, zest and juice
½ tsp freshly ground black pepper

[MAKES 1 JAR]

Place all the ingredients in a large saucepan and heat very gently until the sugar has dissolved. Bring to a simmer and let bubble for 10 minutes until the strawberries start to break down. Transfer to a large sterilized jar and allow to cool completely before sealing and refrigerating. The compote will keep in the fridge for 10 days.

Serve with crusty, buttered bread, swirled through Greek yogurt, or as an ice-cream topper.

*NOTE rosewater and strawberries

For the strawberry ice cream, you may need to use up to
1 tablespoon rosewater depending on the strength. If your
strawberries are very sweet, add a little lemon juice or if they
are more tart, you may want to add a little extra sugar.

This is a perfect winter pudding when there is a dearth of fresh fruit. The cardamom and tea lightly spice the dessert, cutting through the creaminess of the panna cotta.

Cardamom buttermilk panna cotta

with dried fruit compote

[YOU WILL NEED]

oil, for greasing
200ml [scant 1 cup] double [heavy] cream
3 leaves gelatine (or 7g/¼oz powdered
  gelatine)
250g [1 cup] Greek yogurt
25g [1 heaping Tbsp] caster
  [superfine] sugar
5 Tbsp honey
1 vanilla pod [bean], split in half
  lengthways and seeds scraped out
6 cardamom pods, split open and
  seeds bashed

For the compote
150g [5¼oz] mixed dried fruit, such
  as figs, prunes, apricots, sultanas,
  cherries, etc.
300ml [1¼ cups] Earl Grey tea
1 cinnamon stick
1 star anise
1 orange, zest and juice

[SERVES 4]

To make the compote, place all the fruit in a bowl and cover with the tea. Allow to soak for 3 hours, or overnight.

Lightly grease 4 ramekins or dariole moulds with a little oil, then line with clingfilm as smoothly as possible. Heat the cream in a small saucepan, slowly bringing to a simmer. Remove from the heat and allow to cool a little. Soak the gelatine leaves in a small bowl of cold water for about 5 minutes, until soft and jelly-like, then squeeze out any excess water and add to the cream, stirring to dissolve.

Pour the cream mixture into a bowl along with the yogurt, sugar, honey, vanilla seeds and cardamom, and mix well to combine. Divide among the ramekins and refrigerate for at least 4 hours, or until set.

Transfer the soaked fruit and tea to a small saucepan, along with the remaining compote ingredients. Bring to a gentle simmer and cook over a low heat, stirring frequently, for 20 minutes, then strain, reserving the liquid. Discard the spices and reduce the liquid until syrupy before stirring back into the fruit.

Turn out the panna cottas onto plates, gently lifting off the clingfilm. Serve with the warm compote, drizzling with a little leftover syrup.

Rosehips grow in abundance in Sweden and have traditionally been seen as a useful source of nutrients, particularly vitamin C. They were often dried to keep through the winter months and turned into drinks and soups. They have quite a unique, floral flavour – a little like hibiscus – and make for an unusual dessert. If you are lucky enough to get fresh rosehips, you can of course use them for a lighter, more orange-coloured soup. The fresh buds don't need soaking, simply blitz them and cook in boiling water for 20 minutes before straining off the juices. You will need slightly more than the dried variety as they are less concentrated – about 30 per cent more. If you don't fancy the added work of making the cookies, or would like a healthier alternative, simply sprinkle over some roughly chopped almonds.

Rosehip soup

—

with almond cookies & cream

[YOU WILL NEED]

500g [1lb 2oz] dried rosehips
175g [scant 1 cup] caster [superfine] sugar
1 Tbsp cornflour [cornstarch]

For the cookies
100g [3½oz] marzipan
50g [¼ cup] caster [superfine] sugar
25g [1oz] egg whites
200ml [scant 1 cup] double [heavy]
   cream, to serve

[SERVES 4]

Cover the rosehips with 2 litres [8½ cups] water and allow to soak overnight. The next day, pour the rosehips and water into a food processor and blitz to break up the buds. Transfer to a saucepan, cover with a lid and simmer for about 3 hours until you have a thick mush.

Meanwhile, make the cookies. Preheat the oven to 175°C/ 350°F and line a baking sheet with baking parchment. In a food processor, blitz the marzipan and sugar until creamy, then add the egg whites to form a thick paste. Use 2 teaspoons or a piping bag to dot small discs of the mixture onto the baking sheet. Bake for 6–8 minutes, until golden. Allow to cool completely on the baking sheet before peeling off the baking parchment.

For the soup, pass the cooked rosehip mixture into a jug through a fine-mesh sieve, a little at a time, squashing with the back of a spoon as you go, getting as much thick liquid out as possible. Discard the rosehip pulp and measure out the resulting liquid, adding enough water to make up 1.5 litres [6½ cups] of soup. Return to the pan with the sugar and cook over a gentle heat until the sugar has dissolved.

Mix the cornflour with 4 tablespoons of water and add to the soup. Stir until thick. Keep warm while you whip the cream until pillowy. Serve the soup with a dollop of cream and a few almond cookies scattered in for crunch.

This may seem like a surprising combination, but one that works beautifully. Blackcurrants grow in our garden in Sweden and every year my father always makes a tart jam with them for scooping onto ice cream. I will frequently bring a jar or two back to London, sometimes with mixed success. The combination of the journey and improper storage has, on at least two occasions, caused the jam to ferment and the jars to explode, which means a sticky, messy cupboard and a trip to the shops if I want to make this pudding. It's still worth it, though. If you have fresh blackcurrants to hand, do by all means use them to decorate the pavlovas before serving.

Little coffee pavlovas

—

with blackcurrant jam

[YOU WILL NEED]

5 large eggs, whites only, at room
  temperature
300g [1⅔ cups] caster [superfine] sugar
1 Tbsp espresso powder or instant coffee
  granules, crushed to fine powder
2 tsp cornflour [cornstarch]
250-g [8¾-oz] tub mascarpone
400ml [1⅔ cups] double [heavy] cream
2 Tbsp icing [powdered] sugar
1 tsp vanilla extract
3 Tbsp coffee liqueur (optional)
½ jar blackcurrant jam or preserve
cocoa powder, for dusting

[SERVES 8]

Preheat the oven to 120°C/250°F and line a baking sheet with baking parchment. Draw 8 circles, 8–10cm [3¼–4in] in diameter, onto the baking parchment then flip over. Space them out evenly, using 2 baking sheets if necessary.

In a large, clean metal or glass bowl, whisk the egg whites until frothy and peaks start to form. Gradually add the caster sugar, 1 tablespoon at time, until glossy. Whisk in the coffee powder, then add the cornflour. Pile onto the baking sheet circles, swirling as you go.

Bake in the bottom of the oven for 1 hour, until crisp outside and dry on the base, then allow to cool on wire racks.

Beat the mascarpone in a large bowl until smooth, then add the cream. Whisk until thick, then add the icing sugar, vanilla extract and coffee liqueur, if using. Swirl through about half the jam then spoon onto the meringues. Loosen the remaining jam with a little water to a drizzle-able consistency, then drizzle over the pavlovas. Dust with a little cocoa powder and serve immediately.

The spice and orange flavour in this cheesecake are a wonderful combination. Although I originally developed this recipe for Valentine's Day, hearts also frequently feature as Swedish Christmas decorations. It is rather moreish and surprisingly light so I wouldn't begrudge anyone eating it in the summer either. You will need a pipette or dropper for the hearts (available online), but other than that there's no specialist equipment required. Alternatively, you could, of course, simply spread the lingonberry coulis over the top in an even layer for a bright red pop of colour.

Lingonberry & orange cheesecake

———

with a gingersnap crust

[YOU WILL NEED]

200g [7oz] *pepparkakor* (Swedish gingersnap) or ginger cookies, blitzed to a fine crumb
100g [7 Tbsp] unsalted butter, melted
150g [5¼oz] lingonberry or cranberry preserve
2 tsp cornflour [cornstarch] dissolved in 4 tsp water
4 gelatine leaves
300ml [1¼ cups] double [heavy] cream
100g [scant ¾ cup] icing [powdered] sugar
300g [1⅓ cups] cream cheese, room temperature
1 large orange, zest and juice

[SERVES 12]

Line the base of a 24-cm [9-in] loose-bottom cake tin with baking parchment, then, in a bowl, mix the cookie crumbs and melted butter until well combined. Pack the mixture firmly into the tin, spreading out with the back of a spoon so that it is evenly distributed and coming slightly up the sides of the tin. Chill until needed.

Place the preserve in a small bowl and mix with a few tablespoons of water to loosen. Strain through a fine-mesh sieve into a saucepan, making sure to get as much liquid out as possible. Add the dissolved cornflour to the pan and gently heat to a thick but still drizzle-able coulis. Cool completely.

Meanwhile, soak the gelatine leaves in a small bowl of water for 5 minutes until soft and jelly-like. Pour the cream into a pan and bring to a simmer, then immediately remove from the heat. Squeeze any excess water out of the gelatine leaves and add to the warm cream, stirring until dissolved. Allow to cool slightly. Beat the icing sugar into the cream cheese along with the orange zest and juice. Add the cooled cream with 3 tablespoons of the berry coulis and beat until smooth. Pour the cream cheese mixture onto the cookie base.

It's now time to decorate – and for a steady hand! Starting in the centre of the cake, use a pipette to dot tiny circles in a spiral pattern all the way round the cake, letting the dots get bigger as you work your way around. Finally, starting in the middle again, use a cocktail stick to pull through the dots in a continuous, circling motion – try not to lift your hand at all if you can help it. You should end up with a spiral of hearts.

Cover the tin with clingfilm (be careful not to touch the top of the cake!) and chill for 6 hours, or overnight, until set.

Ginger and lingonberry are a match made in dessert heaven and this recipe is a great way to use up that jar of lingonberry jam you may have purchased on a whim at a certain flat-pack furniture store. I appreciate that not everyone has an ice-cream maker – using thick condensed milk and whipped cream is a great way to get the same creamy texture achieved by a machine. The condensed milk is very sweet, so do taste your mixture to make sure you get the balance right – add more ginger if you find it needs it. If you don't have any lingonberry jam to hand, you can use cranberry.

Ginger ice cream

———

with lingonberry jam

[YOU WILL NEED]

500ml [generous 2 cups] double
    [heavy] cream
1 thumb of fresh ginger, peeled and
    roughly chopped
400g [1⅔ cups] canned condensed milk
1 stem ginger ball (from a jar of stem/
    preserved ginger in syrup), finely
    chopped, plus 2 tsp syrup
3 Tbsp lingonberry jam

[MAKES 500ML (1 PINT)]

Heat the cream in a large saucepan, but don't let it boil. Add the roughly chopped fresh ginger and allow to infuse for 1 hour or so until completely cool. Strain into a large bowl and discard the ginger.

Combine the condensed milk with the stem ginger and syrup in another large bowl. Whip the ginger-infused cream to stiff peaks, then add a generous spoonful to the condensed milk. Stir to lighten then gently fold in the remaining cream until well combined. Add 1 tablespoon or so of water to the jam and mix until syrupy.

Transfer the ice-cream mixture to a freezerproof container and swirl through the jam (a knife is a good tool for this), making sure to get all the way down to the bottom. Freeze for at least 6 hours, then bring up to temperature about 20 minutes before serving in scoops.

BAKVERK
[baking]

My earliest baking memories are of my maternal grandmother, or *mormor*. Whenever she came to stay with us in the summer, she would get up at her usual 4A.M., turn the oven on and start making cinnamon buns. The smell would lead me to sneak down to the kitchen sometime around 6 or 7 to watch her sprinkling, folding, twisting and rolling before finally being allowed a first taste before everyone else was awake.

The Swedes love baked goods with a passion that is manifest in the countless *konditori* and cafés that line our streets. The windows bulge with cakes and confectionery with names like Tosca, Tiger, Radio, Hoover, Napoleon and Budapest. Slices of cream cakes, jewel-like marzipan, chocolate bites and, of course, piles of soft cinnamon buns, all to be consumed with copious amounts of coffee – Swedes are among the most voracious coffee consumers in the world.

For us, the act of sitting down to a cup of something warm and a little something sweet is a basic human right. It is such an important part of life that we have even given the act a name – *fika*. This is a not-to-be-messed-with institution, one that is preferable in the company of others (either colleagues, family or friends) but can be grabbed in haste on your own, too. It is often an excuse to slow down and get together, used either as a noun "let's meet for a *fika*" or as a verb "we can *fika* after our walk".

Fika can consist of a cinnamon bun or a couple of cookies, maybe a muffin or a slice of cake if you have something to celebrate. For kids, cordial is often on offer instead of coffee – *fika* covers all tastes and doesn't exclude anyone. And while it could be assumed that with so much preoccupation with baked goods, Sweden is an unhealthy nation, this couldn't be further from the truth. Super-indulgent cakes are not a daily occurrence and treats are set against a backdrop of healthy, balanced eating.

This section is full of recipes, some new and some old, inspired by some of these traditions and principles but also by our favourite ingredients – whole grains, spice, nuts, hearty seasonal fruits and even vegetables.

The later part of the summer was for me always a time of blueberry picking, or rather bilberry picking as these grow on Swedish forest floors in abundance. They are slightly smaller than blueberries and have a distinctive purple centre, which meant that filling a basket took ages and was often a pretty messy process. We'd use them in pies or served simply, sprinkled with sugar in a bowl of cold milk. I love them combined with freshness of lemon balm, which is available throughout the summer months – try finding a plant in your local garden centre. Mint works well as a substitute during the rest of the year.

Blueberry hand pies

——

with demerara sugar & lemon balm

[YOU WILL NEED]

200g [1½ cups] plain [all-purpose] flour
125g [½ cup] unsalted butter, cubed
  and cold
200g [1⅔ cups] fresh blueberries
75g [6 Tbsp] demerara [raw brown]
  sugar, plus 2 Tbsp, for sprinkling
½ lemon, zest and juice
1 small bunch of lemon balm or mint,
  roughly chopped
1 egg, beaten

[MAKES 6]

To make the pastry, pulse the flour and butter with a pinch of salt in a food processor until you have a breadcrumb-like texture. Add 3–4 tablespoons of ice-cold water, 1 tablespoon at a time, until the mixture starts to clump together. Tip out onto a lightly floured work surface and bring together with your hands, then wrap in clingfilm and chill for about 1 hour.

Preheat the oven to 175°C/350°F and line a baking sheet with baking parchment. Mix the blueberries, sugar, lemon zest and juice with the lemon balm or mint.

Roll the dough out to a 30 x 35-cm [12 x 14-in] rectangle. Cut out 6 rough squares and brush the edges with a little water. Divide the blueberry mixture among the squares, sticking mostly to one side, then fold the dough over the blueberries. Press the edges with a fork to seal.

Transfer the pies to the prepared baking sheet and brush with the beaten egg. Sprinkle with the 2 tablespoons of sugar, then snip a little hole in each pie to let any steam escape. Bake for 35 minutes and allow to cool a little before serving.

A really good kladdkaka *(literally meaning messy cake) needs to be properly gooey inside, so do make sure not to overbake it. You can replace the liquorice powder with 2 tablespoons of strong espresso, if desired, which will serve the same purpose – to enhance the chocolate rather than overpower it. If you love liquorice, add more of it in the form of finely chopped soft sweets.*

Kladdkaka

——

[*Gooey chocolate cake with liquorice*]

[YOU WILL NEED]

125g [½ cup] unsalted butter,
    plus a little extra for greasing
2 eggs, beaten
175g [1 cup] caster [superfine] sugar
100g [¾ cup] plain [all-purpose]
    flour, sifted
3 Tbsp cocoa powder, sifted
2 tsp liquorice powder or 1 Tbsp
    strong espresso
50g [1¾oz] soft liquorice sweets [candies]
    (tubes or bars) – not the salted kind! –
    finely chopped (optional)
whipped cream, to serve

[SERVES 8–10]

Preheat the oven to 175°C/350°F. Melt the butter and allow to cool a little. Grease and line the base and sides of a 24-cm [9½-in] loose-bottom cake tin with baking parchment.

Beat the eggs and sugar together with electric beaters until pale and thick, about 2–3 minutes. Add the melted butter, flour, cocoa, liquorice powder or espresso and a pinch of salt. Stir through the chopped liquorice, if using.

Pour the mixture into the prepared cake tin and bake for 15–20 minutes until crisp on top but still gooey in the middle. Serve with whipped cream.

When I was younger, a cluster of rhubarb grew in our garden in Sweden. The stalks were firm, with flushes of pink, at the start of the summer and I was always fascinated by this plant with its huge lily pad-like leaves and edible stems. We baked it, doused in sugar, in simple pie crusts to eat with vanilla whipped cream. This recipe takes things a little further, with almonds for crunch and a wholemeal crust for extra nuttiness. The filling will be pretty wet once cooked so I recommend cooling it completely to allow it to set fully.

Rhubarb meringue tart

with almonds

[YOU WILL NEED]

For the pastry
200g [1½ cups] wholemeal
   [whole-wheat] flour
1 Tbsp caster [granulated] sugar
100g [7 Tbsp] cold butter, cubed

For the filling
1.5kg [3¼lb] rhubarb, cut into
   5-cm/2-in lengths
120g [⅔ cup] caster [superfine] sugar
1 orange, zest
3 Tbsp ground almonds

For the meringue
50g [generous ⅓ cup] blanched almonds
3 egg whites
175g [1 cup] caster [superfine] sugar
3 Tbsp flaked [slivered] almonds

[SERVES 8]

Begin by making the pastry. Place the flour, sugar and butter in a food processor and blitz to a crumb-like texture. Gradually add 3 tablespoons ice-cold water, pulsing between each addition until the mixture comes together into a dough. Shape into a disc, wrap in clingfilm and refrigerate.

Preheat the oven to 160°C/325°F. Tip the rhubarb into a roasting tray, sprinkle with the sugar and orange zest, and bake for 15 minutes until the rhubarb is soft when pierced but still holding together. Remove from the tray onto a wire rack set over a baking sheet to drain, and leave to cool completely.

Roll out the pastry dough to 5mm [¼in] thick and use to line a 22-cm [8½-in] loose-bottom pastry tin. Prick the base all over and return to the fridge for at least 20 minutes.

Increase the oven temperature to 180°C/350°F. Scatter the blanched almonds for the meringue in a roasting tray and toast for 10 minutes until golden, tossing halfway through. Tip onto a board and finely chop. Spread out to cool quickly.

Line the pastry with a circle of crumpled baking parchment and fill with baking beans or rice. Blind bake for 15 minutes, then remove the beans. Bake for 5 minutes more to dry out.

Whisk the egg whites until stiff peaks form. Add the sugar, 1 tablespoon at a time until you have a glossy meringue, then carefully fold through the chopped almonds. Sprinkle the tart case with the ground almonds, then add the rhubarb, piling it up to form an even layer. Spoon the meringue all over, then bake for 30 minutes, sprinkling over the flaked almonds before the last 10 minutes of cooking. Cool before serving.

The appearance of elderflower blossoms is a sure sign that the Swedish summer has arrived after the drawn-out winter and often too-short spring. It grows all through our hedgerows, forests and fields and can be picked at will thanks to our right to roam, known as allemansrätten, *which grants access to wildlife and foraging rights to the whole nation. Elderflower adds a floral freshness to cordials, desserts and in baking – I have even had it in* gravadlax. *It pairs particularly well with nutty coconut in this moist cake.*

Coconut semolina cake

—

with elderflower & pistachios

[YOU WILL NEED]

250ml [1 cup] crème fraîche
300ml [1¼ cups] buttermilk
1 Tbsp baking powder
150g [⅔ cup] unsalted butter, melted
400g [generous 2⅓ cups] semolina
1 tsp vanilla extract or ½ tsp vanilla
    powder or paste
75g [1 cup] desiccated [dry unsweetened]
    coconut
250g [generous 1⅓ cups] caster
    [superfine] sugar
3 tsp elderflower cordial
2 Tbsp pistachios, roughly chopped

[MAKES 16 SLICES]

Preheat the oven to 180°C/360°F and line a 20 x 30-cm [8 x 12-in] high-sided baking tray with parchment. Mix the crème fraîche, buttermilk and baking powder together in a bowl and allow to fizz for a few minutes.

Set aside 4 tablespoons of the mixture and place in a small bowl with the same quantity of melted butter. Mix the semolina, remaining butter, vanilla, coconut and 100g [½ cup] of the sugar together in a large bowl and beat until well combined. Stir in the crème fraîche mixture.

Pour the batter into the prepared baking tray, spreading it out evenly. Top with the reserved buttery crème fraîche and bake for 35 minutes until golden.

Meanwhile, make the elderflower syrup. Place the remaining sugar in a small saucepan with 250ml [1 cup] water and bring to the boil. Reduce the heat to a simmer and let bubble for 15–20 minutes until you have a drizzle-able syrup. Stir through the elderflower cordial and allow to cool a little.

Remove the cake from the oven and test with a skewer or cocktail stick – it should come out clean. Prick all over with a fork, then pour over the syrup. Allow to cool completely before cutting into squares and sprinkling with the chopped pistachios.

This recipe is adapted from Sybil Kapoor's sugar plum tart in Citrus and Spice: A Year of Flavour. *The idea of a yeasted tart dough really appealed to my Swedish baking sensibilities, not least because of the similarity to our own* vetebröd *dough (literally meaning wheat bread), which is the base for cinnamon buns. I have given it a Scandi twist with added cardamom, a nutty crunch from pine nuts and a fragrant perfume of rosemary, which pairs superbly with the apple.*

Apple cake

——

with pine nuts & rosemary

[YOU WILL NEED]

125ml [½ cup] whole milk, plus a little
  extra for brushing
10g [¼oz] fresh yeast
100g [½ cup] golden caster
  [unrefined granulated] sugar
2 Tbsp butter, melted, plus a little extra
  for greasing
1 egg, beaten
300g [about 2¼ cups] plain
  [all-purpose] flour
½ tsp ground cardamom
700g [1½lb] eating apples, cored and
  cut into wedges
1 large rosemary sprig, leaves picked
  and chopped
½ tsp ground cinnamon
2 Tbsp pine nuts

[SERVES 8]

In a small saucepan, heat the milk to "finger warm" (just warm to touch). Crumble the yeast into a large bowl, then pour in a little milk. Stir to dissolve, then whisk in the remaining milk, half of the sugar, the melted butter and the egg.

Add the flour, cardamom and a pinch of salt and beat until the dough starts to come together and pulls away from the sides of the bowl. Tip the dough onto a lightly floured work surface and knead until smooth, about 5 minutes. Return to a clean bowl and cover with a tea towel. Allow to rise in a warmish place for about 1 hour, or until roughly doubled in size.

Grease a 28-cm [11-in] loose-bottom, fluted tart or pie dish. Knock a bit of air out of the dough and then tip it out onto the work surface. Knead for a minute or so then roll out and use to line the pie dish. Prick the base all over with a fork.

Toss the apple wedges with the remaining sugar, rosemary and cinnamon and arrange over the dough case. Allow to prove for about 30 minutes, then brush any exposed dough with a little milk.

Preheat the oven to 200°C/400°F. Sprinkle over the pine nuts and bake for 25 minutes until golden and the apples are cooked.

Parsnip might sound like a peculiar addition to cake, but it's really no stranger than using carrot and that hardly raises an eyebrow. Parsnip, too, will add sweetness and a wonderfully moist texture. However, what I love the most about this cake are the very subtle, earthy tones that balances out the sweet and sour elements.

Parsnip & lemon loaf cake

—

with poppy seeds

[YOU WILL NEED]

150g [generous ¾ cup] caster
   [superfine] sugar
250g [1¾ cups + 2 Tbsp] plain
   [all-purpose] flour
2 tsp baking powder
400g [14oz] parsnips, peeled and grated
2 Tbsp poppy seeds
3 lemons, zest and 2–3 Tbsps juice
150ml [⅔ cup] sunflower oil
100g [7 Tbsp] plain yogurt
4 eggs, beaten
150g [about 1 cup] icing
   [powdered] sugar

[SERVES 8]

Preheat the oven to 175°C/350°F. Grease and line and 900-g/2-lb loaf tin with baking parchment.

In a large bowl, mix the sugar, flour and baking powder together. Add the grated parsnips, poppy seeds and lemon zest, then give everything a really good stir. Pour in the sunflower oil, yogurt and eggs and mix well.

Gently pour the batter into the prepared loaf tin and bake for 50–55 minutes until a cake tester comes out clean. Meanwhile, mix enough of the lemon juice with the icing sugar to make a runny icing. Once the cake has cooled, turn it out of the tin and drizzle over the icing. Allow to set a little before cutting into slices.

KAKOR OCH FIKA

Seven kinds of cookie & the fine art of fika

---

[1] Saffron biscotti with raisins
[2] Jam thumb cookies [*Hallongrottor*]
[3] Chequerboard cookies with vanilla & cocoa
[4] Lotta's caramel cookies with syrup
[5] Margareta's nutty bites with hazelnuts & walnuts
[6] Finnish sticks with almonds & hazelnuts
[7] Chocolate & rye cookies with cardamom

In the days when etiquette and tradition were of utmost importance, a *kafferep* was an excuse for women to get together without husbands or children. The best tablecloths and china would be laid out and several courses of baked goods would be presented. An essential component (after the sponge cakes and buns) was serving seven different kinds of cookies for your guests to choose from – no more and certainly no less.

While baking quite so many cookies is no longer seen as essential in proving your worth as a host, many of the different recipes from this time have endured. The diminutive size make them perfect to have with a cup of coffee for a quick *fika* or to stow in the cupboard for when you have an unexpected guest.

My personal favourites include my lovely Aunt Lotta's caramel cookies,

which were among the first things I ever baked. There were a few summers when I was completely obsessed with them – the penny having dropped that I could combine a few ingredients with the heat of an oven and create something delicious – so we had a constant supply in the cookie jar.

One of my most treasured summer pastimes is to trundle the short walk up the hill to my godparents' house and sit in my godmother Margareta's beautiful, sunny garden with a cup of coffee and her hazelnut bites. It is one of my favourite places in the world and I could while hours away there idly chatting, only moving to stretch for a refill or shoo away her lively (and appropriately named) pug, Cookie.

These recipes will all keep for at least a week or so in the cookie jar.

1. Saffron biscotti

———

with raisins

[YOU WILL NEED]

1 Tbsp milk
pinch of saffron strands
100g [7 tbsp] butter, softened
60g [⅓ cup] caster [superfine] sugar
2 eggs, beaten
1 tsp baking powder
200g [1½ cups] plain [all-purpose] flour
50g [generous ⅓ cup] almonds, roughly
  chopped
50g [⅓ cup] raisins

[MAKES ABOUT 20 COOKIES]

Preheat the oven to 175°C/350°F and line a baking sheet with baking parchment. Heat the milk in a small saucepan or microwave, then add the saffron and allow to infuse.

Beat the butter and sugar with electric beaters for 2–3 minutes until pale and fluffy. Add the eggs, a little at a time, beating well after each addition, then pour in the saffron milk, scraping to get every last red strand. Fold through the baking powder, flour, almonds and raisins to form a sticky dough.

Mould the dough into 3 loaf-like shapes, about 15cm [6in] long and 3–4cm [1¼–1½in] wide and transfer to the prepared baking sheet. Bake for 20–25 minutes until golden. Allow to cool slightly, then slice diagonally into 3-cm [1¼-in] long biscotti. Spread out over the sheet, then return to the oven and turn it off, allowing the cookies to cool and dry out, ideally overnight.

2. Jam thumb cookies

———

[*Hallongrottor*]

[YOU WILL NEED]

200g [¾ cup + 2 Tbsp] butter, softened
60g [⅓ cup] golden caster [unrefined
  granulated] sugar
pinch vanilla of powder or ½ tsp vanilla
  extract or paste
1 tsp baking powder
275g [about 2 cups] plain
  [all-purpose] flour
raspberry jam (about ⅓ of a jar)

[MAKES ABOUT 18 COOKIES]

Preheat the oven to 175°C/350°F and line a baking sheet with baking parchment. In a large bowl, beat all the ingredients, except for the jam, together with a pinch of salt to form a crumbly dough. Roll the dough with your hands into walnut-sized balls and transfer to the prepared baking sheet.

Gently press your thumb into each cookie, taking care so the dough doesn't crack too much. If it does, gently push back together with the palms of your hands. Fill each resulting cavity with about ½ teaspoon of the jam. Bake for 10–15 minutes until golden. Allow to cool on the sheet.

3. Chequerboard cookies

————

with vanilla & cocoa

[YOU WILL NEED]

275g [about 2 cups] plain
    [all-purpose] flour
90g [½ cup] caster [superfine] sugar
200g [¾ cup + 2 Tbsp] butter, softened
pinch of vanilla powder or ½ tsp
    vanilla extract or paste
2 tsp cocoa powder

[MAKES ABOUT 50 COOKIES]

Place half the amounts of flour, sugar and butter into each of 2 medium bowls. In one bowl, stir through the vanilla and in the other beat in the cocoa so it's well dispersed.

On a lightly floured surface, roll each mixture into 2 long sausages, about 1.5cm [⅝in] thick and roughly 30cm [12in] long. Place a length of vanilla dough next to a length of cocoa dough and gently squeeze together. Repeat with the remaining dough and place on top of your first pair, but in the opposite order so the same flavours are placed diagonally. Use your hands to gently squeeze everything together as tightly and neatly as possible, trimming the ends if necessary.

Chill for 30 minutes then preheat the oven to 175°C/350°F and line a baking sheet with baking parchment. Slice the dough into 4-mm [⅙-in] thick cookies and place on the prepared baking sheet. Bake for 10 minutes, then transfer to a wire rack to cool completely.

4. Lotta's caramel cookies

————

with syrup

[YOU WILL NEED]

300g [about 2¼ cups] plain
    [all-purpose] flour
200g [¾ cup + 2 Tbsp] butter, softened
175g [1 cup] caster [superfine] sugar
2 Tbsp golden [light corn] or maple syrup
2 tsp baking powder
pinch of vanilla powder

[MAKES ABOUT 25]

Preheat the oven to 175°C/350°F and line a baking sheet with baking parchment. Mix all the ingredients together in a large bowl.

On a lightly floured surface, roll the dough into finger-thick sausage shapes. Flatten slightly with a fork, then cut on the diagonal and place well spaced out on the prepared baking sheet. Bake for 15–18 minutes, then allow to cool completely on the sheet. If very wide, cut in half lengthways before allowing to cool.

5. Margareta's nutty bites

——

with hazelnuts & walnuts

[YOU WILL NEED]

50g [generous ⅓ cup] walnuts,
    plus 1 Tbsp
50g [generous ⅓ cup] blanched hazelnuts,
    plus 1 Tbsp
100g [½ cup] caster [superfine] sugar
250g [1¾ cups + 2 Tbsp] plain
    [all-purpose] flour
200g [¾ cup + 2 Tbsp] cold unsalted
    butter, cubed
icing [powdered] sugar (optional)

[MAKES ABOUT 25 COOKIES]

Preheat the oven to 175°C/350°F and line a baking sheet with baking parchment. Toast the walnuts and hazelnuts (reserving the extra tablespoon of each) in a dry frying pan until lightly golden, then tip into a food processor with the sugar and blitz until roughly chopped.

Add the flour and butter and pulse until it comes together to form a dough. Roll into 4-cm [1½-in] thick sausage shapes, then chill for 30 minutes.

Carefully slice into 1.5-cm [⅝-in] thick circles and place evenly spaced on the prepared baking sheet. Press a reserved hazelnut or walnut into each cookie.

Bake for 10–12 minutes until golden, then transfer to a wire rack to cool. Dust with icing sugar before serving, if desired.

6. Finnish sticks

——

with almonds & hazelnuts

[YOU WILL NEED]

50g [½ cup] ground almonds
275g [about 2 cups] plain
    [all-purpose] flour
60g [⅓ cup] golden caster
    [unrefined granulated] sugar
200g [¾ cup + 2 Tbsp] butter, softened
1 egg white
2 Tbsp hazelnuts, roughly chopped
demerara [raw brown] sugar,
    for sprinkling

[MAKES ABOUT 25]

Beat the ground almonds, flour, caster sugar and butter together in a large bowl. Chill the dough for 20 minutes.

Preheat the oven to 175°C/350°F and line a baking sheet with baking parchment. On a lightly floured surface, roll the dough into 1.5–2-cm [⅝–¾-in] thick sausages, then cut into 3–4-cm [1¼–1½-in] long "sticks" and transfer to the prepared baking sheet. Brush each with a little egg white, then sprinkle over the chopped hazelnuts and demerara sugar. Bake for 12 minutes until starting to go golden. Allow to cool on a wire rack.

This is the wildcard in the bunch as it's not a classic Swedish recipe but rather inspired by the famous chocolate and rye cookie from the Tartine Bakery in San Francisco. My local favourite, the Brick House in South East London, also do a great version which I have become a bit obsessed with – furiously recipe testing my way forward until I cracked it. I think the nutty rye in these have a distinctly Scandinavian flavour but it wasn't until I had added our other staple, cardamom, that I felt I had really clinched it. The texture is a little unusual with a crispier outside and a soft centre – a sort of cross between a cookie and a brownie.

7. Chocolate & rye cookies

—

with cardamom

[YOU WILL NEED]

400g [14oz] dark [semisweet] chocolate (minimum 70% cocoa solids), broken into pieces
75g [⅓ cup] unsalted butter
75g [¾ cup] rye flour
1 tsp baking powder
1 tsp ground cardamom or 1 Tbsp pods, split and seeds well bashed
4 eggs
200g [1 cup packed] dark muscovado [brown] sugar
1 tsp vanilla extract

[MAKES ABOUT 30 COOKIES]

Melt the chocolate and butter together in a saucepan over a gentle heat. Stir until smooth, then allow to cool slightly. Mix the flour, baking powder, cardamom and a pinch of sea salt together in a small bowl.

In a large bowl, whisk the eggs with electric beaters until pale and full of light bubbles, about 2–3 minutes. Add the sugar, 1 tablespoon at a time, until thick, glossy and caramel coloured, then stir in the vanilla extract. Pour the melted chocolate into the egg mixture and stir to distribute, then tip in the dry ingredients. Combine to form a thick, mousse-like dough, then cover the bowl with clingfilm and chill for at least 30 minutes.

Preheat the oven to 175°C/350°F and line 2 baking sheets with baking parchment. Drop teaspoonfuls of the cookie dough onto the prepared baking sheet, taking care to space them out evenly and flattening slightly. Sprinkle with sea salt and bake for 8–10 minutes. Allow to cool completely on the sheets before diving in.

Known as drottningäpplen *(Queen's apples), this is an easy autumn twist on baked apples. Use your favourite sweet eating apple and you can, of course, use a shop-bought shortcrust pastry for ease.*

Baked apples

---

in shortcrust pastry

[YOU WILL NEED]

150g [1 cup + 2 Tbsp] plain
   [all-purpose] flour
75g [scant ½ cup] golden caster
   [unrefined granulated] sugar,
   plus 2 Tbsp
120g [½ cup] butter, cold and cubed,
   plus 1 Tbsp, softened
1 egg, separated
50g [½ cup] ground almonds
1 tsp ground cinnamon
4 eating apples, cored
ice cream or crème fraîche, to serve

[SERVES 4]

Blitz the flour, the 75g [scant ½ cup] sugar and the 120g [½ cup] butter together in a food processor until you have a crumb-like texture. Add the egg yolk and 1 tablespoon cold water and pulse, scraping down the sides, until the dough starts to clump together. Tip onto a work surface and use your hands to bring the dough together, then wrap in clingfilm and chill for at least 20 minutes.

Meanwhile, preheat the oven to 200°C/400°F. Mix the ground almonds, the 2 tablespoons of sugar, 1 tablespoon of softened butter and the cinnamon together in a small bowl. Use the mixture to fill the apple core cavities.

Roll out the pastry dough on a lightly floured surface until it is 1cm [½in] thick. Divide into 5 square sheets and use 4 to wrap each apple by folding up the corners to meet at the top, trimming off any excess. Squeeze together gently with your hands. Cut the remaining square of pastry into 8 strips. Brush the pastry apples with beaten egg white then use 2 strips of pastry to lay a cross over the top of each apple. Brush over with a little more egg white and transfer to a baking sheet. Bake for 30 minutes until golden. Serve with ice cream or a dollop of crème fraîche.

This recipe is based on an apple cake my mormor *taught me to make that involves cubing apples and scattering over a simple* filmjölk *(a cultured yogurt similar to buttermilk) sponge with lots of cinnamon before baking. She said she used to serve it with cream that had been left to sour slightly – something that was apparently quite a common accompaniment in her day! I have memories of eating it on her veranda, sun warming my legs, on my second or third cup of coffee while* mormor *reminisced about what my mischievous uncles got up to in their teens.*

Pear & ginger traybake

—

with pecan & oat crumble topping

[YOU WILL NEED]

4 eggs, beaten
200g [generous 1 cup] caster [superfine] sugar, plus 1 Tbsp for the crumble
300g [about 2¼ cups] plain [all-purpose] flour, plus 2 Tbsp for the crumble
1 tsp baking powder
1 tsp ground cinnamon
1 tsp ground ginger
1 tsp vanilla extract, or ½ tsp vanilla powder or paste
300ml [1¼ cups] crème fraîche
1 thumb of fresh ginger, peeled and grated
2 Tbsp butter
50g [scant ½ cup] pecans, roughly chopped
20g [scant ¼ cup] porridge oats
3 pears, cored and cut into rough cubes
Greek yogurt or cream (optional), to serve

[MAKES 16 SQUARES]

Preheat the oven to 160°C/320°F. Grease and line a 20 x 30-cm [8 x 12-in] high-sided baking tin with baking parchment. Whisk the eggs and the sugar with electric beaters until light and pale, about 3 minutes. Add the flour, baking powder and spices, then tip in the vanilla, crème fraîche and ginger and beat to form a batter.

Use your hands to rub together the remaining tablespoon of sugar and 2 tablespoons of flour, with the butter, pecans and oats to make a crumble. Pour the batter into the prepared baking tin and top with the cubed pears. Scatter over the crumble mixture.

Bake for 40 minutes until the cake is cooked through and a cake tester comes out clean. Allow to cool a little before removing from the tin and serving still warm with a dollop of yogurt or cream as a dessert. Alternatively, cool completely and serve as a cake.

FIKABRÖD

Four recipes for the best buns

---

[1] *Kanel & kardemummabullar* [cinnamon & cardamom buns]
[2] Blueberry buns with lemon & marzipan
[3] Sticky buns topped with salted caramel
[4] Cranberry & clementine buns with maple & pecans

Often called *fikabröd* (*fika* bread) the cinnamon bun and its ilk form part of a group of cardamom-laced, lightly sweetened, leavened dough called *vetebröd* (literally meaning wheat bread) that are used to make buns, loaves and pastries. There are no limits to the possible fillings, but classics include cinnamon, more cardamom, almond paste, custard, pistachios and apples.

I know the cinnamon bun well. I have made a lot in my time with some disappointing and challenging results. It is humbling knowing I will never make a single batch that can hold a candle to my *mormor*'s incredible versions, but after many years I am pleased with my tried and perfected recipe. The main thing I have learned is not to rush the process. I have tried and failed to make good cinnamon buns when I needed to be somewhere in a few hours or had other things on the stove or in the oven. Take it slow and give these buns their due.

Flour is key. I have decided to use strong white bread flour after a lot of experimenting because I prefer the lighter, airier texture. You could try half strong white/half plain flour for a cakier version or half wholemeal bread flour/half strong white bread flour if you wish; just leave a little more time for the dough to rise and prove. The amount of flour in these bun recipes should be taken with a pinch of salt. It will vary a fair bit depending on the kind of flour you use, even from brand to brand but also from country to country. You may find that you need more or less to get the right results, so add it carefully and vigilantly.

In Sweden, the buns are often sprinkled with something we call pearled sugar (small white crystals) before baking, for extra crunch and sweetness, but as this is hard to find you could brush them with a sugar syrup (see page 158) when just out of the oven and still warm.

Here is the basic recipe for all of the buns in this book. The dough should initially be fairly sticky, but rest assured that it will come together with kneading. This makes a fluffier, more bread-like bun, which is best frozen straight after cooling if you are not planning to eat all the buns immediately. If you want to glaze them with a sugar syrup, bring 75g [6 Tbsp] granulated sugar to a simmer with 100ml [7 Tbsp] water. Let the sugar dissolve and continue to simmer for a few minutes. Allow to cool slightly before brushing over the buns as soon as they come out of the oven.

1. *Kanel & kardemummabullar*

—

[*cinnamon & cardamom buns*]

[YOU WILL NEED]

For the dough
150g [⅔ cup] butter
500ml [generous 2 cups] whole milk
50g [1¾oz] fresh yeast
125g [scant ¾ cup] caster [superfine] sugar
2 tsp ground cardamom or 1½ tsp cardamom pods, split open and seeds bashed
about 800g [5¾ cups] strong white bread flour
1 egg, beaten

For the filling
50g [3½ Tbsp] very soft butter
3 Tbsp caster [superfine] sugar
2 tsp ground cardamom or 1½ tsp cardamom pods, split open and seeds bashed OR 1 Tbsp ground cinnamon (or half of each)

[MAKES ABOUT 22-24]

For the dough, melt the butter in a pan, pour in the milk and heat until "finger warm" (just warm to touch). Crumble the yeast into your largest bowl with a little of the buttery milk. Stir until the yeast has dissolved, then add the remaining liquid. Add the sugar, cardamom and ½ tsp salt, then about 700g [5 cups] of the flour. Mix until you have a wet dough, then tip onto a lightly floured surface and knead to come together. It will be a bit difficult to handle, but moving it vigorously around or slapping and folding it will have an impact. Add a bit more flour if absolutely necessary. Return to a clean bowl and sprinkle with flour. Cover with a tea towel and allow to rise in a warmish place for 1 hour, or until doubled in size. It should now be smooth "like a baby's bottom", as my *mormor* used to say, with a fond pat.

Knock the dough back a bit while still in the bowl, then tip onto a floured surface. Knead for a few minutes, adding more flour if the dough seems very wet. It is ready when it releases from the surface easily and, if you slash into the dough with a very sharp knife, there are evenly distributed small air bubbles. Cut the dough in half and roll each half out to form a rectangle, roughly 30 x 40cm [12 x 16in] and 5mm [¼in] thick, with the longest side facing you. Spread with the softened butter, then sprinkle over the sugar and cardamom or cinnamon (or a combination of both).

Preheat the oven to 225°C/450°F and line several baking sheets with parchment. Roll up each rectangle tightly and slice into even pieces, about 2.5cm [1in] thick. Pinch or tuck in the ends and place, generously spaced, on the prepared sheets. Cover with tea towels and prove for about 40 minutes, until doubled in size.

Brush with the beaten egg and bake for 8–10 minutes until golden. Allow to cool at least a little on a wire rack, or as long as you can wait.

Marzipan features in a lot of Swedish baking and confectionery, particularly as a filling for small cakes and chocolates. In these buns, they lend a sticky sweetness that works brilliantly with the tart blueberries and lemon. Be warned: this is a messy process and the buns may feel quite wet and slippery once they've been filled and cut ready for proving. Don't worry, though – the magic happens in the oven and even if they don't look perfect, they will still taste delicious.

2. Blueberry buns
___

with lemon & marzipan

[YOU WILL NEED]

1 x basic *Kanel & kardemummabullar*
  dough (see page 158)
400g [3¼ cups] fresh blueberries
100g [½ cup] caster [superfine] sugar
1 lemon, zest and juice
50g [3½ Tbsp] butter, softened
175g [6oz] best-quality marzipan,
  coarsely grated
1 egg, beaten

[MAKES 14–16 LARGE BUNS]

Make the basic *Kanel & kardemummabullar* dough according to the instructions on page 158.

While the dough is rising, bring the blueberries, sugar and lemon juice to the boil in a small pan, then lower the heat and simmer for 10–20 minutes (depending on your blueberries), until jammy. Remove from the heat and cool completely.

Line several baking sheets with baking parchment. After leaving the dough to rise, knead and roll it out into 2 rectangles as with the *Kanel & kardemummabullar* recipe. Spread with the butter and blueberry jam, then sprinkle over the marzipan and lemon zest. Roll up and slice into about 14–16 buns in total, then transfer to the prepared baking sheets, cover with tea towels and allow to prove for about 30 minutes.

Preheat the oven to 225°F/450°F. Brush the buns with the beaten egg, then bake for 8–10 minutes, or until golden and puffed up. Allow to cool on a wire rack before tucking in.

This is my nod to the American cinnamon roll – the Swedish cinnamon bun's decadent cousin – which I also love. You could use nuts, like almonds, in the caramel for extra crunch, though I quite like the contrast of pillowy softness with the simple crunch of sea salt.

3. Sticky buns

———

topped with salted caramel

[YOU WILL NEED]

1 x basic *Kanel & kardemummabullar* dough (see page 158)
125g [½ cup + 1 Tbsp] butter, softened
150g [¾ cup] light brown sugar
3 Tbsp golden [light corn] syrup
180ml [¾ cup] double [heavy] cream
50g [generous ⅓ cup] almonds, roughly chopped (optional)
3 tsp ground cinnamon
75g [scant ½ cup] caster [superfine] sugar

[MAKES ABOUT 16-18]

Make the basic *Kanel & kardemummabullar* dough according to the instructions on page 158.

Line a large high-sided baking tin with baking parchment. While the dough is rising, melt half of the butter in a small saucepan, then add the brown sugar and golden syrup. Simmer over a low-medium heat until the sugar has dissolved then add the cream and bring to the boil for 5 minutes. Add a pinch of sea salt and allow to cool until just warm to the touch, tasting to see if more salt is necessary. Sprinkle the almonds, if using, into the prepared baking tin and pour over the caramel sauce, spreading out evenly.

Knead the dough (see page 158), dividing it into 2 rectangles and spreading with the remaining butter, cinnamon and caster sugar. Roll up the rectangles and slice into buns – you should have enough for about 16–18.

Arrange these on top of the caramel, about 1cm [½in] apart. Cover with a tea towel and let prove for 30 minutes.

Preheat the oven to 200°C/400°F. Bake the buns for 15–20 minutes then remove from the oven and allow to cool a little before flipping over. You may find that some of the caramel sticks to the baking parchment, but you should be able to scrape it off and disperse it over the buns. Cool completely on a wire rack set over a baking sheet to catch any dripping caramel, before sprinkling with a little extra sea salt and pulling apart to serve.

I initially made these at Christmas as a way to use up a bag of frozen cranberries, but find myself coming back to them again and again throughout the year. I sometimes substitute the cranberries for fresh lingonberries or even the whole filling with lingonberry jam mixed with a little ginger and clementine juice. Adjust the quantities to your taste; I sometimes want more unctuous buns, so I up the amount of filling.

4. Cranberry & clementine buns

—

with maple & pecans

[YOU WILL NEED]

1 x basic *Kanel & kardemummabullar*
   dough (see page 158)
300g [10½oz] cranberries (fresh
   or frozen)
200ml [⅔ cup] maple syrup, plus 2 Tbsp
3 clementines or 1½ oranges, zest
   and juice
1 tsp ground ginger or ½ tsp grated
   fresh ginger
100g [¾ cup] whole pecans, plus 3 Tbsp
   roughly chopped
1 egg, beaten

[MAKES 14 LARGE BUNS]

Make the basic *Kanel & kardemummabullar* dough according to the instructions on page 158.

While the dough is rising, make the filling. Preheat the oven to 200°C/400°F and lightly oil a baking sheet. Bring the cranberries, 200ml [⅔ cup] of the maple syrup, the orange or clementine juice and zest to the boil in a small pan. Add the ginger and simmer for about 10 minutes until thick and jammy. Allow to cool completely.

Toss the 100g [¾ cup] pecans in the remaining maple syrup and spread onto the prepared baking sheet. Toast in the oven for 10 minutes, tossing halfway. Allow to cool, then roughly chop.

Oil another baking sheet. Divide the dough in half. Roll one half into a roughly 30 x 25-cm [12 x 10-in] rectangle about 2cm [¾in] thick, with the longest side facing towards you. Spread half of the cranberry jam onto the dough and sprinkle with half the maple-toasted pecans. Roll away from you into a sausage-like shape. Using a sharp knife, trim the ends, then slice into about 7–8 buns, each about 5cm [2in] thick. Place on the prepared baking sheet and cover with a tea towel. Repeat with the other half of the dough then allow to prove for about 30 minutes.

Preheat the oven to 225°C/440°F. Lightly brush each bun with a little beaten egg and sprinkle over the roughly chopped pecans before baking for 10–12 minutes until golden and baked through. Allow to cool on a wire rack before tucking in. These are particularly nice halved through their middles and toasted, like teacakes.

These healthy, everyday bread rolls are ideal for breakfast, sandwiches or to mop up soup or stews. Keep a batch at the ready in the freezer and you will feel really quite virtuous and smug.

Spelt rolls

———

with seeds

[YOU WILL NEED]

500ml [generous 2 cups] semi-skimmed [lowfat] milk, plus 2 Tbsp

50g [1¾oz] fresh yeast

3 Tbsp cold-pressed rapeseed oil or olive oil, plus a little extra for greasing

100g [1 cup] porridge oats

25g [scant ¼ cup] flaxseeds, plus a little extra

25g [scant ¼ cup] sunflower seeds, plus a little extra

2 Tbsp honey

150g [scant 1¼ cups] wholemeal [whole-wheat] flour

450g [3½ cups] wholemeal [whole-wheat] spelt flour

[MAKES 20 SMALL BREAD ROLLS]

Heat the milk gently in a pan to "finger warm" (just warm to touch). Crumble the yeast into a large bowl and pour over a little of the warm milk. Stir to dissolve the yeast completely, then pour in the remaining milk and the oil.

Add the oats, seeds, honey and 1 teaspoon salt and stir well to combine. Add the flours, a little at a time, stirring until you have a soft, sticky dough. Tip out onto a lightly floured work surface and knead until the dough comes together, about 5 minutes. Place in a clean bowl, cover with a tea towel and allow to rise for about 1 hour.

Lightly grease 2 baking sheets with oil. Knock the dough back slightly by kneading briefly. Divide and shape into 20 round rolls and place, evenly spaced out, on the prepared baking sheets. Cover with a tea towel and allow to prove for 30 minutes.

Preheat the oven to 200°C/400°F. Brush the rolls with a little milk and sprinkle over the extra seeds. Bake for 12–15 minutes until golden brown and risen. Allow to cool on a wire rack before serving or freezing for later.

These are wonderful to make, as they fill the house with the rich smell of baked rye. They are also completely bulletproof and could probably survive a nuclear attack and still be edible. In an airtight container, they will last for ages and are equally good with cheese, as a canapé base or as a substitute for cereal (see the crispbread recipe on page 28).

The shaping is pretty essential. I favour the more modern rectangular shape which is much more practical in terms of storing and eating: in Sweden the traditional shape is circular and about the size of a dinner plate. These would also have a holes stamped out of their middles, so that you could thread them onto poles to hang up and dry out completely.

Rye crispbreads

—

to have with anything & everything

[YOU WILL NEED]

25g [1oz] fresh yeast
1 Tbsp honey
500g [4½ cups] rye flour
300g [about 2¼ cups] spelt flour
100g [¾ cup] sunflower seeds
50g [generous ⅓ cup] flaxseeds
100g [about ¾ cup] sesame seeds

[MAKES A BIG BATCH;
RECIPE CAN BE HALVED]

Crumble the fresh yeast into a large bowl and add 600ml [2½ cups] "finger warm" (just warm to touch) water. Stir to dissolve then add the honey and 3 tsp salt.

Tip in the rye flour and 200g [1½ cups] of the spelt flour, reserving the rest for later. Mix the seeds together in a small bowl and add half to the dough, then mix together for a few minutes until sticky. Allow to rise in a warmish place for at least 1 hour.

Preheat the oven to 220°C/430°F and line a baking sheet with baking parchment. Divide the dough into 15 pieces and roll into balls. Dust the work surface with some of the reserved spelt flour and roll out each ball into circles, about 5mm [¼in] thick. It will be quite sticky, so do keep dusting with more reserved flour. Make a hole in the centre of each circle (using a small glass or jar) for traditional crispbreads. Or divide the dough into 4, roll into large rectangles and cut into strips about 4 x 15cm [1½ x 6in]. Place onto the prepared baking sheet and dimple each cracker with a fork. Sprinkle with the remaining seeds.

Bake in batches for 10–12 minutes. Once all the batches are done, turn off the oven and pile all the breads onto 2 baking sheets. Put these into the still warm oven and allow to dry out completely for a few hours before eating.

This recipe is a bit like a fruitbread, with the apples lending sweetness, but not so much that this feels like a cake. Toasted, it is fantastic for breakfast spread with cream cheese or salted butter.

Seeded apple bread

—

with honey & thyme

[YOU WILL NEED]

75g [generous ¾ cup] oats
300g [scant 2⅓ cups] wholemeal [whole-wheat] flour
2 tsp bicarbonate of soda [baking soda]
65g [½ cup] flaxseeds
65g [½ cup] blanched hazelnuts, roughly chopped
350g [1½ cups] Greek yogurt
1 egg, beaten
4 Tbsp best-quality honey
2 small eating apples, peeled, cored and cubed
2 thyme sprigs, leaves picked and roughly chopped
2–3 Tbsp mixed seeds, such as pumpkin, sunflower, flaxseeds, sesame – whatever you have to hand
butter, for greasing and to serve

[MAKES 1 LOAF]

Preheat the oven to 175°C/350°F and grease and line a 900-g/2-lb loaf tin with baking parchment. Mix the oats, flour, bicarbonate of soda, flaxseeds and hazelnuts with 1 teaspoon salt together in a large bowl. Stir through the yogurt, egg, honey, apples and thyme.

Pour the mixture into the prepared loaf tin and sprinkle over the mixed seeds. Bake for 1 hour 20 minutes, or until a cocktail stick comes out clean. If the loaf is going too brown but not yet cooked through, cover with foil and continue baking. Remove from the oven and allow to cool completely before slicing and serving spread with butter.

SMÅTT OCH GOTT
[bits & bobs]

There was a time, before importing food from afar became the norm, when certain periods of the year were particularly challenging for Swedes. There would be little to nothing growing in our farms and fields and the countryside could easily be covered with snow from late autumn into spring, particularly in the north.

In order to survive, weather-hardened Swedes became master preservers, using recipes and techniques passed down through the generations. Berries and fruits were turned into jams, cordials and chutneys, and vegetables were pickled and brined as well as placed in adequate cold stores.

We also developed ways to make meat and fish last longer. Smoking, pickling and curing meat and fish became commonplace and are used in many of our favourite dishes to this day. In particular, curing salmon for *gravadlax* (literally meaning "buried fish", as it was kept in the ground to keep cool) is a favourite dish to prepare for guests.

Nowadays, these techniques and recipes are often reserved for celebrations – a whole side of salmon is difficult to get through on your own. While picking fruit for jams and cordials may perhaps not be an everyday activity, it is certainly considered a fairly typical weekend pastime for the family.

The recipes in this section are full of ideas for extending the seasons, but also contain a few extra bits and bobs – such as a popcorn snack (great for "cosy Friday") and some drinks.

Aquavit is a common spirit throughout Scandinavia and, while it used to be one of the most popular ways to consume alcohol, these days it is more usually brought out during traditional festivities like Midsummer, Christmas and Easter. There are even specific songs to sing when downing a shot; the lyrics to the most famous one basically translates as "down in one!".

The dominant flavours in aquavit are always based on dill and caraway, but there are many different varieties that can also be infused with other herbs (fennel and anise are popular), citrus and even flowers (my favourite is an elderflower version). I like my cocktails strong, bitter or spicy rather than fragrant or sweet, but I find the heady spices in aquavit work well with the freshness of mint in a julep – it's a great way to use up that bottle between holidays.

Swedish mint julep

——

with aquavit

[YOU WILL NEED]

1 small bunch of mint, 2 bushy sprigs
   reserved
2 tsp caster [superfine] sugar
150ml [⅔ cup] aquavit, such as O.P.
   Anderson

[SERVES 2]

Divide the bunch of mint and sugar between 2 glasses. Lightly crush the mint with a muddler or spoon. Top with lots of crushed ice and pour over the aquavit. Stir well, then top with more ice and garnish with the mint sprigs.

PRESERVED FISH

Smoking, salting, pickling & curing

---

[1] *Gravadlax* with pomegranate
[2] Pickled prawns with a mustard & chilli kick
[3] Smoked prawns with quick chilli mayo
[4] Smoked mackerel with lapsang souchong

Out of all of the preserving that we Swedes do, conserving fish must surely hold the highest position. Whenever there were guests to entertain, parties to be held or holidays to celebrate, this would be the time for *gravadlax*, pickled herring in a range of flavours, and smoked fish and seafood. Christmas, New Year's, Easter and Midsummer tables are not quite the same without a selection to choose from.

Then there is, of course, *surströmming*, literally "sour herring". You might have heard about these bulging cans of fermented herring with their strong smell (so strong, in fact, that many believe it is illegal to open them in public places). Contrary to popular belief, this isn't something that Swedes indulge in all that frequently; in fact, I'd venture to say that most haven't even tried it. The more common ways we enjoy preserved fish are much more palatable (and legal). As the saying goes, *surströmming* is the only fish that is harder to eat than to catch.

Nonetheless, I can appreciate that the idea of preserving fish may seem intimidating, but rest assured that it is perfectly safe and not nearly as difficult as it sounds. I have included a few of my favourite recipes here which show off the fish in all its glory.

I particularly love juicy, smoked prawns [shrimp] with a simple dip, ideal for eating outside on a balmy summer's evening. Always use the best-quality, freshest fish you can find – ask your fishmonger for assistance.

"Surströmming: den enda fisken som är svårare att äta än att fånga"
["Sour herring: the only fish that is harder to eat than to catch"]
SWEDISH SAYING

1. *Gravadlax*

——

with pomegranate

[YOU WILL NEED]

2 pomegranates, halved
3 Tbsp caster [superfine] sugar
1 tsp white peppercorns
3 Tbsp sea salt
1 small bunch of dill, finely chopped,
    plus extra to serve
1 small bunch of mint, finely chopped,
    plus extra to serve
500g [18oz] sushi-grade salmon fillet,
    skin-on
crème fraîche, to serve

[SERVES 3-4 AS A STARTER]

Halve the pomegranates and put on an apron (this is not a job for your favourite white top!). Set a large sieve over a bowl and break up the pomegranates, squashing a bit to release the juice. Reserve the pomegranate seeds.

Mix the sugar, peppercorns, sea salt and the herbs with the pomegranate juice. Line a baking sheet with plenty of cling film. Place the salmon on top and cover with the pomegranate mixture. Fold up the cling film and wrap in another layer. Place the tray in the fridge, weighed down with a few cans, for 2 days, turning every so often and draining off any excess liquid.

Remove the cling film and brush off any excess herbs and spices. Thinly slice the salmon and scatter with the reserved pomegranate seeds, mint and dill. Serve with crème fraîche.

----

2. Pickled prawns

——

with a mustard & chilli kick

[YOU WILL NEED]

400g [14oz] cooked tiger or Atlantic
    prawns [shrimp]

For the pickle
4 spring onions [scallions], thinly sliced
50ml [3½ Tbsp] cold-pressed rapeseed oil
    or olive oil
4 bay leaves
4 garlic cloves, sliced
1 tsp mustard seeds
1 tsp fennel seeds
1 tsp crushed red chilli (red pepper) flakes
1 lemon, zest and juice
1 celery stick, diced
150ml [⅔ cup] white wine vinegar

[SERVES 4 AS A STARTER]

Mix all the ingredients for the pickle together in a large jug. Pour over the prawns and leave in the fridge for 24 hours before serving in shot glasses as a canapé. Alternatively, serve on buttered toast as a starter or for a light lunch.

*NOTE smoking

The smoking times in this recipe will vary depending on the size of your prawns – Atlantic prawns will be quicker whereas fat tiger prawns can take double the amount of time.

If you have a stovetop smoker or are able to use your barbecue as a hot smoker, this is a great recipe. However, I'm going to go ahead and assume that you don't. Please remember to keep your kitchen really well ventilated when doing this, all doors and windows open, and remember that any textiles in your kitchen might get a bit fishy or smoky.

3. Smoked prawns

with quick chilli mayo

[YOU WILL NEED]

100g [½ cup] sea salt

50g [¼ cup] sugar

500g [1lb 2oz] uncooked prawns [shrimp], such as Atlantic or tiger, shell on

1 good handful of wood chips, like oak, apple or cherry (do not use hickory)

For the quick chilli mayo

2 Tbsp mayonnaise

4 Tbsp crème fraîche

½ lime, zest and juice

½ tsp smoked paprika

1 tsp sweet chilli sauce or ½ tsp chipotle paste

[SERVES 2]

Begin by brining the prawns. In a large bowl, mix the salt and sugar together in 1.5 litres [6½ cups] water. Stir until dissolved then add the prawns and refrigerate for about 30–40 minutes.

Remove the prawns from the brine and pat completely dry.

Set up your smoker. Line a large wok with a very generous layer of foil with lots of overhang all around. Add the wood chips to one side of the wok. Sit a wire rack on top of the wok, ideally one that just fits, and place the prawns on the rack on the opposite side to the wood chips. Top with a lid and seal the sides with the overhanging foil, using more if necessary to seal tightly, so that no smoke can escape.

Place the wok over a medium heat and let the prawns smoke for about 10 minutes. When done, remove the foil and open the wok – I prefer to do this outside as there will be a lot of smoke.

Mix all the ingredients for the chilli mayo together in a small bowl and season with salt and pepper. Serve straight away while the prawns are still warm, or refrigerate the prawns and mayo and serve cold.

Mackerel is one of the easiest things to smoke at home and get great results as the smoky flavour works so well with this oily fish. Using tea leaves mixed with rice instead of wood chips adds an extra layer of delicate flavour. I've gone for a classic smoky tea in this recipe, but you could try experimenting with green tea or camomile. Serve with a potato salad and some leaves to make it the star of the show or use it to top some toasted and buttered rye bread with a squeeze of lemon.

4. Smoked mackerel

with lapsang souchong

[YOU WILL NEED]

4 mackerel fillets, skin on and pin-boned
   (get your fishmonger to do this for you)
100g [½ cup] rice
2 Tbsp Demerara [raw brown] or light
   brown sugar
1 Tbsp tea leaves, ideally a smoky tea like
   lapsang souchong or green tea

[SERVES 4]

Begin by salting the mackerel. Sprinkle a plate or tray with 1 tablespoon sea salt, place the mackerel on top, then sprinkle over another tablespoon of salt. Leave for 10 minutes, then brush off any excess salt and pat completely dry.

Line a large wok with foil as for the Smoked Prawns recipe on page 177. Mix the rice, sugar and tea leaves together in a small bowl, then tip this into the wok. Place the mackerel on a wire rack set over the rice mixture. Cover with a lid and wrap all around the sides with more foil.

Place the wok over a medium heat and let the mackerel smoke for about 15 minutes. When done, take the wok outside, remove the foil and open to let out all the smoke without setting off your fire alarm.

Serve warm with a potato salad or leave to cool and serve with salad leaves, beetroot and a horseradish dressing.

Plums grow in our garden in Sweden, but the trees are so old and temperamental, it's hit and miss as to whether they will fruit or not. When they do, we make the most of the precious crop by preserving them. This is a dark, rich autumnal condiment that is perfect with meat, especially bacon or sausage sandwiches. However, it also works well as a chutney for cheese.

Plum ketchup

―

to serve with meat or cheese

[YOU WILL NEED]

500g [1lb 2oz] plums, pitted and
    roughly chopped
250g [8¾oz] ripe tomatoes,
    roughly chopped
4 garlic cloves, roughly chopped
2 red chillies, deseeded and
    roughly chopped
250g [1¼ cups] dark brown sugar
200ml [scant 1 cup] red wine vinegar
3 Tbsp balsamic vinegar
2 Tbsp fish sauce
2 star anise
1 cinnamon stick

[MAKES 2 BOTTLES]

Tip all but a handful of the chopped plums and half of the tomatoes in a large saucepan. Add the garlic and chillies and bring to a gentle simmer for 20 minutes, until the tomatoes and plums have collapsed. Transfer to a food processor and blitz until smooth.

Return the purée to the pan, bring to the boil and add the remaining plums and tomatoes, sugar, vinegars, fish sauce and spices. Let it bubble for about 40 minutes, stirring frequently. Remove the star anise and cinnamon and pour into 2 sterilized bottles.

Allow to cool completely before sealing and keeping in a cool, dry spot for up to 2 months. Once opened, the ketchup will keep in the fridge for 3 weeks.

I remember my university friends Tom and Pete coming to Sweden for a visit one summer and being particularly amused by the prevalence of dill. While I must stress that it isn't the only herb we use with abundance, it's true that we have embraced it a bit more vehemently than most other nations. Dill makes a lovely fresh addition to almost anything – even snacks. Try this recipe for lemon and dill popcorn for starters and see if you don't agree.

Lemon & dill popcorn

—

for sharing [or not]

[YOU WILL NEED]

3 Tbsp butter
1 lemon, zest
2 tsp dried dill
2 Tbsp vegetable oil
100g [½ cup] popcorn kernels

[MAKES 1 LARGE BOWL]

Melt the butter in a small saucepan with the lemon zest and dried dill. Set aside but keep warm so that the butter doesn't solidify.

Heat the oil in a large saucepan over a medium heat with a few popcorn kernels. Once they have popped, the oil is hot enough, so immediately tip in the remaining kernels. Partially cover with a lid, allowing a little steam to escape. I use a glass lid so that I can see how the popcorn is doing plus it's quite fun watching it pop. Shake the pan frequently and wait until there are about 5 seconds between pops before removing from the heat and tipping into a large bowl.

While the popcorn is still warm, drizzle over the lemon and dill butter and sprinkle with plenty of sea salt. Toss really well to evenly distribute and serve straight away.

PICKLED HERRING

Three simple ways

---

[1] Curried herring with chives
[2] Apple herring with leek & parsley
[3] Ginger & orange herring with dill & mint

[ALL RECIPES SERVE 2 AS A MAIN MEAL, OR 4 AS A STARTER
OR AS PART OF A SELECTION OF PICKLED HERRINGS]

Here comes a confession. I have never pickled my own herring. I have watched others do it, seen the effort and work that goes into it, but I have never tried it myself. To be honest, I don't know many Swedes who have. What is much more common is to buy lightly pickled herring and then add flavours to it. This may seem like cheating, but the quality of a lot of pickled herring is really good and, in my opinion, much more reliable than the quality of fresh herring outside Scandinavia. You can buy pickled herring for further pickling (sounds strange, but true). This is ready preserved without any flavourings, essentially a blank canvas for you to add your own brine and then mix with sauce of your choice; we call these pickling herring or 5-minute herring. However, these can be difficult to find, so my suggestion would be to get a ready-pickled plain version (often with onions, carrots and peppercorns in the brine) and add the sauce of your liking. Leave the flavours to infuse for a few hours or overnight before serving.

In Sweden, we have two types of herring: *strömming* and *sill*. They are often confused by visitors, but basically they are the same type of fish, just found in slightly different places. *Strömming* is found on the east coast and because of the low levels of salt in the waters there, are slightly smaller than *sill*, which is fished off the southern and western coasts. *Sill* is probably the closest thing to the larger Atlantic herring found in the UK and what we tend to use for pickling.

I have had a lot of different flavours of pickled herring, including teriyaki! It is a surprisingly rich dish. You could serve a selection as a starter to a Swedish-inspired supper, or quite easily turn them into a full meal by adding some boiled potatoes with lots of butter and dill, crispbread and a selection of cheeses. Here are three of my favourite ways to make pickled herring.

1. Curried herring

———

with chives

[YOU WILL NEED]

1 jar (about 240g/8½oz) plain
   pickled herring
100g [7 Tbsp] crème fraîche
3 Tbsp mayonnaise
½ lemon, zest and juice
2 tsp medium curry powder
1 small bunch of chives
½ red onion, finely chopped

Drain the herring and remove any bits of vegetables or spices.

Mix the crème fraîche, mayonnaise, lemon zest and juice together in a large bowl. Add the curry powder and most of the chives, then fold through the herring.

Refrigerate for a few hours, then serve topped with the remaining chives and red onion.

2. Apple herring

———

with leek & parsley

[YOU WILL NEED]

1 Tbsp olive oil
1 leek, finely sliced
100g [7 Tbsp] crème fraîche
75g [⅓ cup] light mayonnaise
2 apples, cored and finely chopped, with a
   few wedges chopped into matchsticks
1 small bunch of curly parsley, finely
   chopped
2 Tbsp apple juice
1 jar (about 240g/8½oz) plain
   pickled herring
few dill sprigs, to serve

Heat the oil in a pan and lightly fry the leek for a few minutes, until just starting to wilt but still retaining all of its colour. Spread the leek out onto a plate to cool completely.

Mix the crème fraîche, mayonnaise, leek, chopped apples and parsley together in a large bowl. Stir in the apple juice and season with salt and pepper. Drain the herring, discarding any bits of carrot, onion, spices, etc.

Add to the sauce, then refrigerate for a few hours, or overnight, before serving sprinkled with dill and the apple matchsticks.

Fresh flavours, like herbs, spice and citrus, are often added to herring marinades as they work so well with the richness of the fish. The orange and ginger here don't dominate at all, rather they just add a delicate hint of flavour. For stronger results, you can leave the herring to marinate for a little longer or overnight.

3. Ginger & orange herring

with dill & mint

[YOU WILL NEED]

1 jar (about 240g/8½oz) plain
   pickled herring
1 orange
1 small thumb of fresh ginger,
   peeled and grated
1 small bunch of dill, roughly chopped
1 small bunch of mint, roughly chopped

Set a sieve over a wide jug or bowl and drain the herring, reserving the pickling liquid.

Use a sharp knife to peel the orange, avoiding the bitter white pith. Finely chop the peel and add to the liquid. Squeeze the orange and add the juice to the liquid with the grated ginger. Remove the herring from the sieve, avoiding any bits of vegetable or herbs and add the fish to the pickling liquid.

Refrigerate for a few hours and then serve sprinkled with the fresh herbs.

Elderflower snaps

made with vodka or gin

[YOU WILL NEED]

6–8 elderflower heads
1 lemon
1 Tbsp caster [superfine] sugar
70ml [2½fl oz] vodka or gin

[SERVES 1]

Trim any large bits of stem from the elderflower and discard any brown flowers (or bugs!). Place in a large sterilized jar. Peel the lemon with a small paring knife, avoiding any white pith. Add the peel to the flowers along with the sugar. Pour over the vodka or gin, seal the jar and shake to dissolve the sugar.

Place in a cool, shady spot for a week, tipping the jar upside down every time you walk by or remember. Sieve the snaps and serve neat with lots of ice or with tonic water and a slice of lime for a refreshing take on a G&T.

Cherry jam

with star anise

[YOU WILL NEED]

1.2kg [2½lb] cherries (any variety), fresh
    or frozen, pitted and roughly chopped
500g [2¾ cups] jam sugar (or caster/
    superfine sugar plus 2 tsp pectin)
2 star anise
½ lemon, juice

[MAKES 1 JAR]

Tip the roughly chopped cherries into a large saucepan with the sugar, star anise and lemon juice and a splash of water. Bring to the boil, then reduce the heat and simmer gently for 15–20 minutes until thick and jammy. Try the wrinkle test on page 25 to see if it's ready.

Pour into a sterilized jar and allow to cool a little before sealing. The jam will keep in the fridge for several months.

Index

ACKNOWLEDGEMENTS

This book would not have happened if it wasn't for a host of dedicated, hard-working women. Thanks must first go to my agent *Lauren Clarke* at Bell Lomax Moreton for her enthusiasm, unfailing encouragement and vision – thanks so much for persevering with my scrambled ideas and managing to see a clear path when I couldn't! *Céline Hughes* and the whole team at Quadrille for their dedication to bringing this book together and for so heartfully believing in it from the get-go… and for putting up with every missed deadline. Thanks also to *Gemma Hayden* for your wonderful design which manages to somehow feel incredibly modern and at the same time totally timeless – how did you manage that?! *Harriet Webster* and *Harriet Butt* for all your patience and hard work. *Yuki Sugiura* for your eye for detail and for going above and beyond to ensure this book is filled with the most beautiful photographs. You made every shoot day a pleasure! *Linda Berlin* for all the gorgeous props that set the tone and tied everything together. It was wonderful to have another Swede on the shoot – not least for the great taste in Scandi pop! Thank you to my assistants – *Jenna Leitner* for your organization and meticulous eye and *Laurie Perry* your tireless energy. There's not a chance I would have been able to style this book without you both. Thank you to *Faith Mason* for her images for this book's proposal. *William Rose Butchers* and *Moxon's Fish* on Lordship Lane for getting me odd cuts and herring in the midst of a national shortage. To *Twin Earth Ceramics* for the lovely plate on our cover. The phenomenal women of *Lips Choir* for your encouragement and enthusiasm. You inspire me to be braver and go for things even when I think I can't or shouldn't, one Thursday evening at a time. A massive "tack" must also go to the women who motivated me to get in the kitchen in the first place and whose recipes feature in this book: *Mamma, Mormor, Lotta* and *Margareta*. Thank you to the photographers and stylists whom I've had the pleasure of working with and who egged me along on what would otherwise have felt like a very treacherous path. To name a few: *Emily Jonzen, Kris Kirkham, Emily Kydd, Adrian Lawrence, Laura Lesslie, Debby Lewis-Harrison* and *Rob Streeter*. *Rosana McPhee* at Style Department for your patience and understanding when I was too busy to take on styling work. *Kate, Craig* and *Rosalia* for cheering me on when I (literally) left my keys and closed the door on the art world to embrace something new. Thank you to the herd for being the best biffers. *Emily Kerr* – thank you for the hours spent designing my very first book proposal, and for all your interest and unfailing cheer. *Kate Fisher* for all the lengthy chats dissecting the ups and downs and always insisting all this is worth doing. This book is dedicated to my *mormor, Thorborg (Tobbe)* who is as fearless as she is a wonderful cook. *Tack mormor för alla recept och för att du alltid tyckt att köket är ett ställe som är värt att vara i.* It is also for *Toby* who puts up with me when I'm tearing my hair out, with cancelled commitments and with a kitchen frequently off limits and yet holds my hand throughout. For believing that the world rewards the willing explorer even if it means we often have to take the longest, most challenging routes. There would be no book without you. And finally to the *littlest bear*, who was with me when this book was written and photographed but I have yet to meet. You'll be out a month or so before this book and we'll make every effort to ensure you are born into a *lagom* life, though I suspect it might all be a bit more hectic – apologies in advance.

PUBLISHING DIRECTOR: Sarah Lavelle
CREATIVE DIRECTOR: Helen Lewis
COMMISSIONING EDITOR: Céline Hughes
EDITORIAL ASSISTANTS: Harriet Webster and Harriet Butt
DESIGN AND ART DIRECTION: Gemma Hayden
PHOTOGRAPHY: Yuki Sugiura
PROP STYLIST: Linda Berlin
FOOD STYLIST: Steffi Knowles-Dellner
FOOD STYLIST ASSISTANTS: Jenna Leiter and Laurie Perry
PRODUCTION CONTROLLER: Tom Moore
PRODUCTION DIRECTOR: Vincent Smith

COVER CREDIT: "Neapolitan" plate by Katerina Syriou,
creator of Twin Earth Ceramics

First published in 2017 by
Quadrille Publishing Limited
Pentagon House
52–54 Southwark Street
London SE1 1UN
www.quadrille.com

Quadrille is an imprint of Hardie Grant | www.hardiegrant.com

Text © Steffi Knowles-Dellner 2017
Photography © Yuki Sugiura 2017
Design and layout © Quadrille Publishing Limited 2017

Cataloguing in Publication Data: a
catalogue record for this book is
available from the British Library.

ISBN: 978 1 78713 037 1

Printed in China